the creative era

between the testaments / carl g. howie

ALETHEIA

$1.45

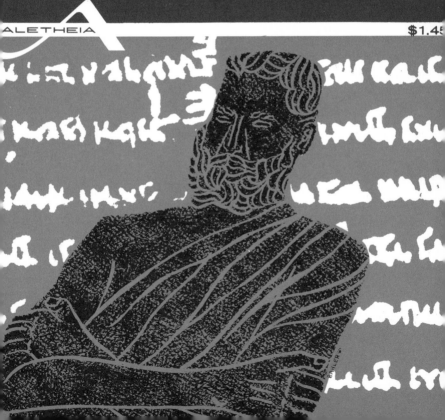

THE CREATIVE ERA

THE CREATIVE ERA

Between the Testaments

1344

CARL G. HOWIE

JOHN KNOX PRESS
Richmond, Virginia

Library of Congress Catalog Card Number: 65-10117

© M. E. Bratcher 1965

Printed in the United States of America

2073(WB)6902

DEDICATION

to

John Bright

scholar, teacher,

and friend

in appreciation

Contents

Introduction

The period between the Old and New Testaments is a blank for most laymen as well as many clergymen who are otherwise well versed in the historical background of the Bible. This is true largely because the Old Testament account leaves off in the period of Ezra-Nehemiah so far as clear historical account goes. Daniel, while written later, is historically set in the sixth century B.C. within the framework of the Neo-Babylonian Empire. Readers therefore tend to jump over more than four centuries from Ezra to the earliest New Testament writings. Most people erroneously assume that little of significance happened during the blank period of time.

In point of fact this era was most active politically, intellectually, and spiritually. The Persians came and went; the Greeks rose to leave their indelible imprint upon the minds of men. They in turn were followed by the Romans who came to stay in the Middle East.

Demons and angels filled the ether; light and darkness struggled for man's loyalty. Seven archangels were balanced by many demons in man's conception of the unseen, and life became conflict on a high level. In the world, parties and sects were formed until there was fragmentation of the Jews into Pharisees, Sadducees, Essenes, Zealots, and others. It was an active, creative era both in the one world of political struggle and in the fragmented world of man's inner life. The Maccabees won their revolt and established a free Israel. Priestly office and princely power were combined in one man, but hope was lifted above the sphere of human accomplishment. Essenes withdrew to the desert and one colony of that party flourished at Qumran where the Dead Sea Scrolls were produced. In due course the Romans came to take the land and ultimately to decimate the Essenes at Qumran.

When Jesus appeared, the world was vastly different from the world Ezra knew. Much happened in those four centuries, and one must understand those happenings if he wishes to comprehend the meaning of the New Testament. For those in whose minds there is a gap in knowledge of the period, this book is presented.

Thanks to the discovery of the Dead Sea Scrolls and other materials, we are in a much better position to understand the minds of faithful people in that era. One can now trace the shadow and substance of faith as they conceived it. Comparison of pseudepigraphical and apocryphal materials with the newly found manuscripts yields a clearer picture of the era just prior to the Christian era.

The period of time with which we deal was a creative era in which God was active and man was responsive. Fixed positions in faith and life were in flux, and within that changing framework one senses the creative spirit of God brooding over a new chaos. In due course, out of this disordered situation, partly because of it, God brought the new creation in Jesus Christ. Not every event or idea of this period can be called creative, but the general changing atmosphere induced a response of creative thought and action in faithful people. Therefore, this era is one of the most significant in human history and in God's providence it served to prepare for the coming of Christ.

Carl G. Howie

San Francisco
July 24, 1964

I

HISTORY IN MOTION

Policy of Cyrus

When the right man and the right moment meet, history is made. To be sure, history is the moving story of man, a restless creature who thrives on change but pursues security. Cyrus the Great rose in the mid-sixth century B.C. to institute a period of change and to give promise of security. The moment came for him in 550 B.C. when the old Chaldean Empire was disintegrating from within. Gifted with military genius, he successfully pressed his campaign of conquest until at last he conquered Babylon in 539 B.C. The star of Cyrus had risen; change had begun and the forms of security were being refashioned.

Cyrus' military power was supreme; his political authority went unchallenged. He was therefore free both to extend his conquest abroad and to make policy innovations at home. His first major policy shift altered the long-standing imperial attitude toward freedom of movement and worship for captive peoples.

The Assyrians as early as the eighth century B.C. had forbidden or discouraged national cults in favor of victorious Assyrian gods. Part of the fruits of victory, according to the Assyrians, was the elevation of their national deity to supremacy over conquered people. The Assyrians also interchanged vast numbers of people from one area to another. This particular policy was designed to forestall any attempt at revolution by people of the same national background, since most rebellions had some semblance of holy war and were connected to a national god. For military and political reasons the Assyrians mixed the people and restricted free religious practice. Freedom of movement and of worship were never rights given captive peoples under either the Assyrians or the Chaldeans.

Cyrus, no longer threatened by political rebellions or fearful of national gods, established new policies in the Medo-Persian Empire. His historic edict granted toleration to all religious groups in their native settings.[1] He honored Marduk in Babylon and recognized Yahweh as the God of the Hebrew people (Ezra 1:1-5). The edict of religious toleration, as contained in Ezra, was literarily shaped by Jewish presuppositions, but it accurately reflects the intent of the great king who followed this new policy for practical and political reasons.

Jews Return to Build

Both Cyrus and his son Cambyses encouraged captive peoples to return to their homeland, if indeed they wanted to go back. Under provisions of the royal decree, Sheshbazzar, who was appointed governor of the Jerusalem area, and his company of fellow Jews left Babylon for Jerusalem during the reign of Cyrus. The immediate purpose of their return in 538 B.C. was to restore the Temple (Ezra 1:5-11). However, little progress was made on the project for seventeen or eighteen years. Nor did the venture prove successful until vigorous leadership arose.

Fortunately such leaders did arise. Zerubbabel, who followed Sheshbazzar as leader of the Jewish community, joined with Joshua the high priest in moving the people to get on with the job. However, it took the words of Haggai the prophet to light the fuse of action in the year 520 B.C. (Ezra 3:1-13).

Even so, the times were not settled nor was the situation secure. Following the death of Cambyses, the Persian Empire was torn by violent strife and rocked with uncertainty for about four years as struggle for royal succession developed. During this unsettled time Zerubbabel was proclaimed king-messiah by Haggai (Hag. 2:1-5; Zech. 4:7-10). Unhappily the unsettled condition in international affairs was mistaken by the prophets as evidence that God had set his people free. It is possible that Zerubbabel undertook some independent and rebellious course during the uncertain era.² In any case, when Darius I emerged in 518 B.C. as absolute and unchallenged ruler, Zerubbabel was at least de-throned if not either imprisoned or executed outright.³

During the reign of Darius I, the second Temple of the Jews was erected under the leadership of Zerubbabel and Joshua, to-gether with the prophets Haggai and Zechariah.

Two sermons by Haggai in 520 B.C., the year work began, pro-vided the needed impetus for determined action among the peo-ple (cf. Hag. 1:1–2:9). In 515 B.C., amid great rejoicing, the Temple was finished and dedicated to Yahweh. Proper worship was reinstituted in Jerusalem after an interruption of some sev-enty years. While the second Temple could not be compared in grandeur with the first, it provided a needed center for the present and a hope for the future restitution of national life. The Jewish people were home again and were at least free to worship God in the sacred spot where Yahweh came to meet them.

Major patterns of history in the larger ancient world were ap-parently influenced very little by the happenings in and around Jerusalem. The course of the empire moved on but Judah re-mained a quiet little island in the midst of a Persian sea of power. Darius I died in 486 B.C., having tasted defeat at the hands of the Greeks in the battle of Marathon (490 B.C.). He was succeeded by Xerxes I, who also tried without success to subdue the Greeks. Xerxes did force the pass of Thermopylae in 480 B.C. over the dead bodies of Leonidas and his warriors, only to sustain a devas-tating naval defeat at Salamis. Persian efforts against the Greeks were notably unsuccessful, but in due course the Greeks would appear on the Persian scene.⁴

These shifting events were part of the total atmosphere of change in the world at that time, making the intertestamental period a creative era in both faith and life.

Nehemiah and Ezra

Artaxerxes I succeeded to the throne in 464 B.C. and ruled un-til 424 B.C. His reign coincided with many stirring events in the history of the Jews who had returned to the Jerusalem area.

Apparently a kind of euphoria settled on the Jews at Susa, the
Persian capital, after the early days of Persian rule. Since the
people of God had been allowed to return home, it was assumed
that all the purposes of homecoming had been carried out. Actually there was little active interest among the exiles in the state
of affairs in the homeland. But for Nehemiah, a courtier and eu-
nuch at Susa, this happy unconcern was shattered by an eyewit-
ness report from Jerusalem. The Temple had been built as
planned, but the Law was neither known nor kept, proper sacrifices were not made, tithes were seldom paid, and the walls of the
city were still in ruins. Nehemiah, shocked by the report, got royal
permission from Artaxerxes I to go to Jerusalem. He felt that the
walls of the city must be restored; it was unthinkable to leave the
Temple unprotected.

He arrived in Jerusalem about 440 B.C. and began to survey
the desolate situation. His efforts attracted first the attention and
then the opposition of local petty rulers who were threatened by
the prospect of a fortified city rebuilt among them. At the outset
they wanted to share in the project but Nehemiah would have
none of it. Three antagonists were Sanballat, a devotee of Yahweh
and governor of Samaria; Tobiah, commander of the Ammon; and
Geshem, who had authority over Edom and parts of Arabia.
They turned to other means and methods. Threat, subversion, and
blackmail were employed. Needless to say, their efforts failed and
Nehemiah's labor force, always ready for military attack, re-
paired the breaches in the walls in fifty-two days; under the circumstances that must have set some record for determination.
The city was secure from attack and the finishing touches on the
walls were completed at a more leisurely pace within two years
and four months. The job was done by 437 B.C.

Nehemiah was a determined man endowed with organizational skill so he accomplished what he had come to do without
appreciable delay. Final completion of the walls was marked by a
most exuberant celebration (Neh. 12). Another step toward the
restoration of faith and community to Israel had been taken.

But Nehemiah discovered that the needs of the people were
not met by protective walls. Internal changes were required; re-

form was necessary. Intermarriage threatened the purity of faith. Sabbath laws were not kept and usury was widely practiced. The tithes and offerings of the Temple were improperly handled. Nehemiah as resident governor did much to correct these conditions among the people, but true reform of life and faith was accomplished by Ezra, the ready scribe and lawgiver. Ezra, who appeared so suddenly, is usually dated before Nehmiah in the year 458 B.C. which is the seventh year of Artaxerxes I. It appears, however, that Nehemiah and Ezra were contemporaries in Jerusalem, and that their efforts complement each other especially in the area of religious reform. Conditions in which Ezra found the city upon arrival argue strongly for his coming after Nehemiah had finished his first term as governor, hence the most tenable date for Ezra would be 428 B.C. after the first twelve-year term of Nehemiah, the governor. A scribal error accounts for the faulty chronology.[5]

Nehemiah returned to the court in Persia after twelve years as governor. However, following a brief stay at Susa, he came back to Jerusalem to resume his duties. Meanwhile, Ezra was appointed to undertake a thorough religious reform in Jerusalem. In fact it is possible that Nehemiah arranged for Ezra's appointment. To fulfill his mission, Ezra was granted both power and funds by the king to use at his discretion in carrying out needed reform among the people according to their law. Artaxerxes I also invested Ezra with authority to enforce his decisions once they were made (cf. Ezra 7:11-24).

After arrival in Jerusalem, Ezra spent three days getting settled. The fourth day was set aside for the dedication of gifts brought from Persia to the Temple (Ezra 8:30-34), and that was followed by a huge public sacrifice honoring Yahweh on the occasion of life renewed under God's Law. With these preliminaries complete, Ezra got down to the business at hand. A wooden platform was built upon which he stood to read and to interpret the Law of God to the people (Neh. 8:8). The reading of the Law was met by a mixture of popular gloom and joy—gloom over failure to keep the Law and joy over having recovered it.

The most glaring problem that had arisen in the Jewish com-

munity at Jerusalem, as Nehemiah discovered, was mixed marriages. Living in the midst of other peoples, youths in Jerusalem
habitually married outside the faith. Such unions tended to com-
promise faith in the name of tolerance. Ezra decreed that these
marriages be annulled and no further intermarriage be allowed.
His orders were carried out and intermarriage, according to the
record, was expunged from the life of the people (cf. Ezra 10).

Ezra built the wall of the Law around the people and Nehemiah erected a wall of stone to protect the city. One was designed
to shut out ideas and the other was raised as a defense against in-
vaders. Both were defensive in purpose but each was somewhat
static by nature. Neither fulfilled completely the purpose for
which it was intended. Truth tended to become crystallized and
was reduced to definitions and boiled down to dogmas among
the Jews. Righteousness was thought out in terms of rules and
right doctrine. Ezra and Nehemiah elevated their homeland to a
good, defensive position and set the course for its future. Jews became thereafter largely a people of the Law, of rules and regulations. Perhaps this was necessary for an interim period but in the
long view it almost smothered the vital spirit of creative faith.

Judaism was locked into the political power structure of Persia and nobody after Zerubbabel seemed to challenge or question
this unhappy fact of political life. Nehemiah was himself part of
the court of a Gentile empire. The story of Esther and the book
of Tobit reflect Jewish involvement in Gentile affairs. On the
broad world stage the Jewish people accommodated themselves to
Gentile domination, but on the narrow scene of Judah and Jerusalem they stood aloof from all foreign intrusion.

Rise of Greece

Persia's imperial power had only a century to run when Ezra
arrived in Jerusalem, although to the contemporary observer the
empire looked permanent. This impression was common with the
Jews of the time who were unaware of Greek stirrings in south-
ern Europe. But like the Neo-Babylonian Empire (Chaldean)
which Cyrus destroyed, the Persian monolith had become old and
weak. Its days were almost ended.[6]

Meanwhile to the north, Philip II ascended the throne of Macedonia in 359 B.C. By 338 B.C. he had extended his power over all the Greek city-states and other principalities of the Greek peninsula. A military general of no mean skill, he is mainly remembered as the father of Alexander the Great, who succeeded to his throne in 336 B.C. Credit belongs to Philip for bringing the noted philosopher and teacher Aristotle to his court to tutor his precocious son Alexander. The parental decision about the education of his son changed the course of world history, making Alexander not only a unique conqueror but equipping him to become patron of a cultural revolution. Wherever Greek arms went, Greek ideas were firmly implanted.

Alexander moved eastward in 334 B.C. to the Granicus River where, using his disciplined phalanx against unwieldy Persian military formations, he decisively defeated the Persians. The next year at the battle of Issus (333 B.C.) Alexander sealed the fate of Palestine and Egypt which were soon conquered. The coup de grace was administered to the dying body of the Persian Empire in 331 B.C. far to the East at Gaugamela, where all organized opposition ceased. In a period of less than four years Alexander demolished the Persians and undermined Persian cultural influence in the Middle East, but the empire did not break up into pieces; it remained intact under new direction and was enlarged by the vigorous action of Alexander.

Driven by an insatiable desire for conquest and for the spread of Greek enlightenment, Alexander advanced to the borders of India. At the pinnacle of his military success in 323 B.C. he died leaving only an infant son as his successor. The empire quickly broke into warring factions, each led by a member of Alexander's able staff of generals.

Jews Under the Ptolemies

In due time a Greek general named Ptolemy established himself in Egypt, and Seleucus, another general, served as his subordinate. However, Seleucus soon broke from under Ptolemaic dominance in 311 B.C. to establish his own independent dynasty which was centered in the Syro-Mesopotamian area. Happily the Jews

were left under the protection of the more benevolent Ptolemies
but their eventual fate hinged on the outcome of conflicts between
the Ptolemies and the Seleucids. Inevitably the old tug-of-war began between these two powers with Palestine as prize. By 302
B.C. the contest became acute. War and intrigue continued until
272 B.C. with little advantage to one side or the other. Palestine
and its Jewish inhabitants were pawns in a deadly international
chess game. At length, Egypt, under the Ptolemies, gained and
held tenuous control of Palestine for more than a century. However, with the rise of Antiochus III to Seleucid power, the tide began to turn. Although his initial military forays into Syria and
Palestine in 221 B.C. and 219 B.C. did not succeed, he was not to be
put off permanently. Inconclusive battles gave the Egyptian army
time to regroup and reorganize. Therefore the next test of strength
proved temporarily disastrous for Antiochus III at Raphia
where Ptolemy IV was completely victorious in battle. Syria and
Palestine remained part of Egyptian territory until 203 B.C. when
a change of Egyptian rulers gave Antiochus his chance. The struggle began and lasted for about five years. Ptolemy V, a mere child
who succeeded his father, was no match for the Seleucids who
won a decisive battle at Panium in 198 B.C., ending Ptolemaic
control of Palestine. That prize now passed over into Seleucid
hands. This proved to be a major historic shift with tragic consequences for the Jews in Palestine.

So far as we know, the Jews in Jerusalem fared well under
Ptolemaic rule. During this time the Hebrew Law and other
Scriptures were translated into Greek for use of Jewish communities in the Greek cultural setting. Jews were free to pursue their
religious and social practices in accordance with policies established by the Persians. There was little interference and no record of brutality. Hence later Jewish literature never inveighed
against the oppression of Ptolemaic rule.

Toleration became so general that the Jewish people possibly
accepted it as a normative condition for kindred elements in the
Middle East two centuries before Christ. Actually, clash between
the Seleucids and Ptolemies on the one hand and the Jews on the
other was inevitable. It is easy to forget that though these political

states were located in the Middle East their point of view was Greek. Their meeting with the Jews was not the encounter of similar people with variant viewpoints; it had deeper roots and more lasting implications. Alexander had initiated a cultural revolution which inspired many adherents with an evangelistic fervor for enlightenment of the world. The Greek way was to them the way of the future; everything must give in before it. Mental agility and logical perspective were combined with a new freedom of life and a different understanding of nature. The Greek way was a challenge to Hebrew faith whether backed up by force or not. Two world views met; two different faiths struggled for the central loyalty of men.

Jews Under the Seleucids

Antiochus III apparently did little to change the broad and tolerant policy established by his Ptolemaic predecessors. His main interests were military but his campaigns ran afoul of the Romans at Magnesia in 190 B.C. His freedom of action and that of his successors was seriously limited by Roman power which was beginning to assert itself in the Middle East. In 187 B.C. Antiochus III was killed while sacking the Temple at Elymais. His successor, Seleucus IV, continued to keep hands off the Jewish enclave which was allowed to continue as an exception to an otherwise pan-Greek policy.

These shifts in political power and military position were quickly followed by religious consequences. That situation was complicated when the office of the high priesthood was sold to the highest bidder early in the reign of Antiochus IV. Jason bought it for a fee and took the place of Onias. Later Antiochus deposed Jason in favor of Menelaus, the next highest bidder, who assumed the highest and holiest office of the Jews. Not only did Menelaus depose Jason; he also had Onias, the legitimate high priest, killed.

But Jason was far from dead. In fact, while Antiochus was campaigning in Egypt (169 B.C.) Jason re-established himself as high priest in Jerusalem, deposing Menelaus, the royal appointee.

Upon returning, Antiochus kicked Jason out and reappointed Menelaus. The high priesthood had become an office to be used at the whim of the king. But the people had had enough. The high priesthood was neither to be sold to the highest bidder nor to be treated as another political prize. These people were not willing to be subservient to a priest neither ordained of God nor in line of historic priestly succession. They therefore rebelled against the latest manipulation of ecclesiastical office.

Revolt led to reprisal. In 168 B.C. Antiochus IV, called Epiphanes, proscribed the practice of the Jewish worship and faith in all its forms. Circumcision was forbidden as was possession of the Torah. Sacrifices to Yahweh were suspended at the Temple; there was no high priest. In fact, the Temple was rededicated to Zeus Olympus and sacrifices were made to him. Official worship of Yahweh at the Temple ceased by order of the Syrian king.

This action of Antiochus Epiphanes probably stemmed from a number of causes. First his plans of conquest in Egypt had been thwarted by Roman intervention which frustrated his hope for expansion. While Antiochus was away, Jason had the temerity to take over the high priest's office from which the king had dismissed him. Add to this the people's refusal to accept Menelaus as their high priest, and Antiochus' interpretation of these events as outright rebellion is understandable. In fact, he faced both religious and political rebellion.

In fairness it should be said also that Antiochus IV was motivated by real zeal for the Greek way of life in opposition to Hebrew faith. He doubtless felt that the advantages of intellectualism should be shared with these people who had walked so long in the strange darkness of their ancient faith. According to Greek thought, logical analysis, not divine revelation, was the key to the nature of life; man should be much more concerned with the nature of life and creation than with its source. Fables and myths about the gods were cast aside as the Greeks became free from superstitions and mores of the past. Antiochus hoped to give this new outlook to all the backward people of his region. In fact he thought that he was divinely chosen to carry out the missionary task. Zeus was the same god, more perfectly understood, as Yahweh; why not merge the two? Antiochus must have reasoned that the marks of difference between Jew and Greek were circumcision, the Law, and sacrifice. Remove these differences and, he thought, the problem would be solved.

This position taken by the king had many adherents among the Jewish avant-garde. Even before Antiochus started his program, some Jews sought his permission to build a gymnasium in Jerusalem. Youths were attracted by Greek games in which the participants ran in the nude and where the exuberant vigor of youth was freely expressed. Greek relaxation of restraint appealed to the young people of the land. It became fashionable to remove the marks of circumcision and to wear hats with brims in Greek style. To be up-to-date meant to ape Greek ways and to engage in Greek thought.

For these and other reasons Antiochus took a calculated risk. Once the decision was made, he pressed his program with unrelenting vigor. A strange ceremony, repeated at various towns and other centers of life, marked the inauguration of the new faith in a community. An officer of the government would appear in the town or village and prepare to make a sacrifice. The sacrificial animal used to honor Zeus was a pig, to the Jews the most despised of all domestic animals. When all was in readiness, a local Jewish volunteer was requested to kill the sacrifice. Once the act of worship was finished, the official Greek cult was thought to be established. Thus the new way was being quickly and insidiously introduced from village to village across the countryside. The tide was running to Greek culture. Assimilation of the new ways endangered the ancient faith in a historic God who required men not to follow nature but to obey him. The struggle involved far more than cult practices and social mores; it involved a way of life.

The Maccabean Revolt

The Antiochian reform went very well since most Jews avoided contact by withdrawal or silent noncompliance, but the program struck a real snag at the town of Modein in the hill country northwest of Jerusalem. There the ceremony reached the point at which a Jew was asked to volunteer to make the sacrifice. Mattathias, a priest, was invited to participate in sacrifice but he refused. Immediately another Jew stepped forward to comply. The act was never completed because Mattathias, filled with rage, killed both the Jew and the Syrian officer who had charge of inaugurating religious reform in Modein. Mattathias raised the banner of open revolt against the Syrians, saying: "Let every one who is zealous for the law and supports the covenant come out with me!" (1 Mac. 2:27b). Not only did these guerillas attack Syrian forces; they punished apostate Jews as the enemies of God. Disorder followed.

Since Mattathias was an old man at the beginning of the revolt, nature cut short his participation in it. He died a natural death in 166 B.C. and was buried by his five sons: Judas, Eleazar, John, Jonathan, and Simon. Judas, the natural leader of the brethren, took leadership of the revolution, succeeding his father. Within a few months he had become a legendary figure who assumed the surname or nickname "Maccabeus," meaning "Hammerer." History remembered Judas Maccabeus and called this war for independence the Maccabean Revolt.

Judas trained and organized his troops well so that he had considerable success in his first engagements with Syrian armies. This was true not only because Judas was both courageous and intrepid, but also because the Syrians at first did not take the revolt seriously. As result Judas defeated and killed Apollonius who was sent out against him; he ambushed a large troop of Syrians at Beth-horon, causing a general retreat by the enemy. Moreover, Gorgias, another Syrian general, fared little better against the tough Jewish warriors who numbered some 3,000.

After these initial Jewish victories, Lysias, who had been left in command while Antiochus IV was away on a military campaign, took direct action himself against Judas at Beth-zur, south of Jerusalem. The battle that followed was a standoff leading to negotiations between the two military leaders. Peace was concluded. Terms provided in part for Jewish reoccupation of Jerusalem and reinstitution of worship at the Temple. After proper cleansing, restitution of worship was fully accomplished on December 25, 165 B.C.

The Jews had been without proper worship or acceptable sacrifice from three to three and a half years. This trial for the holy ones was especially agonizing since they believed that strict adherence to Law and making of sacrifice were commanded by Yahweh. Judas Maccabeus threw off the yoke of oppression in an amazingly short time. He gained for his people freedom of conscience and of religious practices. To his Jewish contemporaries, that in itself was a miracle which they credited to Yahweh's power and grace.

Despite Judas' victories and the concessions made to him, the Syrians maintained military control of Acra, the fortified high point in Jerusalem. Syrian troops continued to be garrisoned there. This situation remained unchanged until the death of Antiochus IV provided for Judas the ideal moment to attack Acra. Once more Judas and Lysias faced each other on the field of battle. This time Lysias decisively defeated Judas and lifted the siege of Acra. He also destroyed the fortifications of the Temple and forced the Jews to accept his terms of peace. However, freedom of religion was confirmed as a principle, and Temple worship was allowed to continue.

Seleucid succession and power were uncertain, hence the dynasty was always in danger of collapse. Kings and pretenders seemed to come from all quarters. Demetrius I, a claimant to the throne, escaped from Rome where he was held prisoner. Upon arrival in Syria he became king, having executed his predecessor, Antiochus V. Alcimus, a thoroughly Grecianized Jew, was appointed high priest, over the protests of the Hasidim. Therefore when Judas withdrew his forces from Jerusalem, Alcimus wreaked vengance upon the Hasidim. After his bloody act of retaliation he remained alive and in power only because Demetrius protected him.

While these ghoulish events went on in the city, the Syrian king dispatched a military column to Jerusalem under command of Nicanor, but Judas intercepted and defeated the troops at Adasa. He took possession of Jerusalem and the Temple again.

Thus Judas held both political and religious authority in his own hands by 162 B.C. Finally Demetrius, determined to end this irritating and puzzling revolution, dispatched his general Bacchides who met, defeated, and killed Judas at Elasa in 160 B.C.

The Hasmonean Dynasty

With the death of Judas, however, the revolt reached a crisis and a turning point. The tide of battle and the fact of defeat left the Maccabean partisans in a difficult position. All the gains of Maccabean effort appeared at the moment to be in jeopardy, if not entirely lost. Jonathan, a brother of Judas, who succeeded to the leadership of the Maccabean Revolt, retreated into the wilderness of Tekoa, out of Syrian reach. There he bided his time until more favorable circumstances provided him a chance to act. Meanwhile, guerilla activity would suffice. Alcimus continued to refashion religious practices in Jerusalem along Grecian lines. Earlier political and religious reforms were more than offset by the counter-reform of the Greek-minded high priest. There was little that the Maccabean leader could do about the trend. Jonathan, though an effective guerilla leader, was not strong enough to challenge Syrian control. In due course, when it was to the advantage of both sides, Jonathan made peace with Bacchides in 158 B.C. For five years the land was at peace until Seleucid dynastic troubles disrupted the calm and drew Jonathan into the resultant turmoil and intrigue. Then the revolutionary Jew became part of the system against which he had fought. This represented, not subservience, but accommodation. In any case, one can date the disintegration of the Maccabean spirit of revolt with this peace of Jonathan.

Demetrius I, hard put to maintain his power against the challenge of the imposter Alexander Balas, turned for help in his distress to Jonathan, giving him in return authority to raise troops and to free hostages in Jerusalem. As a result all Syrian garrisons, except for those at Acra and Beth-zur, were withdrawn from Jonathan's domain. For benefits received, Jonathan was expected to support Demetrius. Jonathan the brilliant revolutionary was now a political intriguer. He sold his soul for a mess of pottage.

Not principle but expediency motivated Jonathan who supported Alexander Balas in exchange for royal confirmation of Jonathan's claim to both civil and sacred offices. Jonathan took the mantle of high priest in 153 B.C. and remained loyal to Alexander, his benefactor. This choice was fortunate since Demetrius I was defeated and died in battle in 150 B.C. In the long view, however, the expedient choice proved that Jonathan was not to be trusted. He was now committed to the dangerous game of power politics in which stakes are high and results uncertain. Moreover he alienated many of his own people by both wearing the crown and taking the office of high priest. Ambition, not principle, dictated action.

In the waning years of the Seleucid Empire no new ruler, including Alexander Balas, was long secure. In 145 B.C. Demetrius II claimed the throne. Unfortunately, Jonathan, mistaking the signs of the times, remained loyal to his benefactor Alexander Balas, who was assassinated in 145 B.C. The rest of the details of intrigue and power struggle need not detain us. Jonathan became independent both politically and militarily at the dangerous price of involvement in the dynastic struggles of the Seleucids.

In 143 B.C., a victim of counter-intrigue, Jonathan was captured and imprisoned by Trypho, a Syrian general. Simon, brother of Jonathan, tried unsuccessfully to obtain his brother's release. Trypho murdered Jonathan in prison and assassinated the Seleucid monarch Antiochus VI as well. He then had himself proclaimed king over the remaining Seleucid shell of power.

Simon, the last survivor of the five sons of Mattathias, took full power over the Temple and palace in Jerusalem after the death of his brother. He captured Acra in Jerusalem and wiped out the last vestige of Seleucid domination and control. Seleucid power declined in all quarters and Simon was quick to step into the vacuum. He was not only ruler, but the people, who no longer objected to the dual role, made him high priest as well. The rule of the Hasmoneans began in 142 B.C. when the country was free from outside domination.[7] Simon beat back every challenge to his power on the field of military conflict, but he, like Jonathan, was not well-favored in the game of political intrigue. His own son-in-law assassinated him and two of his sons, but John Hyrcanus, another son, in Gazara at the time of the royal assassination, escaped death to become high priest and prince. His rule began quietly, but far from brilliantly, in 134 B.C. The development from revolution to dynasty had come full circle; the Hasmoneans, though home grown, were no improvement over the Seleucids. In about 130 B.C. the Syrian king Antiochus VII attacked Jerusalem, forcing Hyrcanus to surrender and setting a very high indemnity on the city. However, the death of Antiochus VII permitted Hyrcanus to resume independent rule. Dynastic uncertainty, political ineptitude, and military weakness on the part of the Seleucids allowed Hyrcanus to consolidate his power. When he died in 104 B.C. and was succeeded by Aristobulus (104-103 B.C.), the land was secure.

Upon his rise to power, Aristobulus imprisoned his brothers, but after his death, Alexandra, his widow, freed them and forthwith married the eldest, Alexander Janneus (103-76 B.C.). Militarily, Alexander Janneus was too ambitious for his own good. He attacked Ptolemais and was saved from disaster by the intervention of Cleopatra III. He then turned his efforts to Transjordan and thence back to Philistia. This young king was always busy with attempted military conquest; however, his efforts in early years were seldom crowned with success. Alexander was neither a brilliant nor an idealistic revolutionary; he was another ambitious petty ruler, who took advantage of the situation.

In 94 B.C. Alexander's army came to grief in an invasion of Transjordan where the Nabatean king Obador would not countenance Jewish intrusion into the areas of Moab and Edom. Most of the Jewish army was destroyed in the field. Rebellion broke out in Jerusalem, and the rebels, hiring Demetrius III, Eucerus, to lead them, defeated Alexander decisively in 88 B.C. Alexander was dethroned and made a fugitive. Remembering earlier days, the Jews sympathized with their deposed king, now bereft of power and a wanderer in the desert. As a result six thousand Jews went over to his side, enabling him to re-establish his throne. Bloody reprisals followed his return to power.

In a complicated three-way military struggle between the Nabateans, the Syrians, and the Jews, Aretas the Nabatean king emerged victorious. Peace with the Nabateans, while frustrating the southward march of a restless and ambitious Alexander, freed him to move militarily in other directions. He moved with such success that when he died in 76 B.C. he ruled over territory almost as extensive as the empire of Solomon. But the days of Hasmonean power were numbered and Maccabean glory was forgotten.

Alexandra succeeded her husband and as queen elevated her eldest son Hyrcanus II to the office of high priest. She reigned in peace and the land prospered (76-67 B.C.), but externally during her reign the shadow of Rome fell more insistently across the Jewish future, and internally the Pharisees became a powerful force. The Pharisees were probably a liberalized outgrowth of the Hasidim who earlier supported the Maccabean Revolt. During the reign of Alexander Janneus, it was probably they that fomented revolt against the king. Growth of Pharisaism also became a major influence on the internal shape of things to come.

The Rise of Rome

Rome waited for the chaotic situation to reach a crescendo before stepping in as the arbiter of law and order. That moment of crisis came when the Hasmonean dynasty petered out under Aristobulus II. Hyrcanus II was deposed as high priest and allowed to retire to private life, but Aretas, the Nabatean king, offered to elevate Hyrcanus to the throne. War between the brothers resulted. Aristobulus, defeated by Aretas and deserted by his own troops, retreated to the Temple.

At that juncture the Roman commander-in-chief Pompey forced Aretas to lift the siege that had been laid on Jerusalem and confirmed Aristobulus in power for the moment. In 63 B.C. Pompey in Damascus listened to the rival parties and to representatives of the Jewish people. Jerusalem was taken, the throne was toppled, and Hyrcanus II was confirmed as high priest. Political independence for the Jews ended with the coming of the Romans, but freedom of conscience and religious practice were left nearly inviolate. The early purposes of the Maccabean Revolt were firmly fixed.

This period of political change and social upheaval provided the atmosphere for reassessment and for new understanding. God was at work in the minds of men which were made sensitive by the uncertainty of the times. Revolution and counter-revolution followed both in Rome and in Palestine. When the smoke of uncertainty cleared, Herod the Great had become king of the Jews (37-4 B.C.). The son of Antipater, an Idumean, this troubled and bloodthirsty despot pursued a vigorous policy which brooked no rival to Roman power. When Octavian (Caesar Augustus) emerged from Roman civil war as emperor, he confirmed Herod's position as king and gradually increased the size of his territory.

Herod was of great value to Rome, restoring order out of chaos in the Middle East. Even so, the unseen inner disorder created in the minds of men was not settled or satisfied by the Pax Romana or by the power of a repressive Herod. Man's certainty had been troubled and he was open to a new basis for certainty. Unaware of the unseen struggle of faith, Herod engaged in some remarkable and lavish building projects which were of momentary significance. The most important structure which he erected was the third Temple of the Jews, which was begun in 20 B.C. but was not actually finished until several decades after his death. While other aspects of faith were creatively in flux, the Temple stood as an awesome bastion of the status quo. More of significance was happening in the synagogue and other religious centers than at the Temple.

King Herod died an embittered man, but one who had used power ruthlessly, killing off his own family but remaining loyal to Rome and keeping the imperial peace among the Jews. Palestine had become part of the burgeoning Roman Empire in the Augustan era. The disappointing Hasmonean house was in shambles, but the Maccabean spirit of revolt lived on among the Jews. Some Jews wanted only religious autonomy, but others, the spiritual descendants of the Maccabees, aspired to complete political autonomy. Others were looking for a renewal in faith and were open to the leading of God in a new day.

The tortuous trail of history had come to a climactic point when Jesus of Nazareth was born. One of the most confused and yet one of the truly creative eras in human history was climaxed by his coming. God had set the stage in Palestine and in the ancient world. Upheaval is always the atmosphere in which creative events occur and creative ideas are given voice. Stirring events were matched by movement of spirit and mind in those days which we shall seek to describe briefly in the pages of this book.

II

THE RECORDS

Primary source material from which information and evidence about the intertestamental period can be drawn is more extensive than might first appear. Several books of the Old Testament bear directly on the subject and events at hand, and, in fact, all of the Old Testament influences the shape of events and the color of attitudes developed within the period.

In addition, the fourteen or fifteen books of the Apocrypha fill out in more detail the substance of faith and the condition of life in those days. First Maccabees, for example, is a source for massive authentic information about the Maccabean Revolt, while Ecclesiasticus, or the Wisdom of Jesus the Son of Sirach, supplies additional evidence for understanding of manners and morals of the time. These two works trace the thread of external events and the less concrete development of faith and culture.

The Pseudepigrapha ("false writings") has generally been neglected by students and writers concerned with the intertestamental period. Actually this amorphous collection is probably the best source for understanding the plasticity and creativity of the situation during the last two centuries before Christ. Books such as the Testaments of the Twelve Patriarchs and Enoch are invaluable sources of information. In them it is possible to trace the rise and development of many ideas and doctrines which otherwise appear to leap full-grown onto the New Testament scene, e.g., demonology, angelology, heaven, and hell. Moreover, pseudepigraphical literature also developed a detailed legalism for practically every aspect of life and at the same time raised man's hopes above the historical scene to apocalyptic vision.

Another rich primary literary source began to become available to scholars in 1947. The so-called Dead Sea Scrolls, discovered in and around the Qumran plateau, provide a wealth of material for the researcher and writer in this field. To be sure, some of the manuscripts found were texts of Old Testament books—Isaiah, Samuel, Deuteronomy, etc.—together with copies of books of the Apocrypha and Pseudepigrapha. But manuscripts discovered in the fifteen scroll-producing caves have also included midrashim (commentaries), doctrinal materials, and new books of psalms and liturgies.

This vast material is still in process of discovery, collation, transcription, and translation, but it has already revolutionized our understanding of the period from 125 B.C. to A.D. 68.

Finally, it is evident that Josephus, a Jewish historian who became a Roman citizen, and Philo, a philosopher, are to be listed as secondary sources. Josephus' works are not to be accepted uncritically but neither can they be ignored.[1]

The Old Testament

The Old Testament, including the Law and the Prophets, but not all the so-called Writings, was widely accepted de facto as canonical after the time of Ezra, even though formal canonization had not occurred. Study of and comment on the Law became a primary function of religious leaders, especially the scribes. Wisdom and Law were merged by wise men and scribes. Temple cult and the elevation of the Law began to take precedence over prophetic utterance in religious experience. Many parts of Scripture were recast in the light of legal and cult requirements (cf. Jubilees). Therefore, the whole Old Testament forms a backdrop for the intertestamental period, or in particular the last two centuries B.C.

Of more immediate interest, however, are the books of Ezra, Esther, Ecclesiastes, Daniel, parts of Zechariah (9-14), and the book of Jonah.

Ezra reflects that element of thought in the emerging situation which insisted upon a strict legalism as the sum and substance of faith. Absolute separation from the Gentiles was a first requirement of true religion according to Ezra and his succes-

sors. Exact fulfillment of the Law in every detail was the way
of righteousness which caused the creation of detailed codes
and prescriptions for the good life.

Contrary views were at loose in the world of the Jews. Esther is a book in which the heroine and Mordecai were very
much at home in the Persian court. Esther, by marriage and apparently with God's blessing, was herself integrated into the
Persian scene, displacing Vashti, the queen. She was favored by
Ahaseurus and was delivered by God from the plot of anti-
Jewish Haman. This story represents a far more tolerant approach to the Gentile world than Ezra did. Although probably
written in the late Persian period, Esther is a historical novel
which affected the shape of events and ideas in the two centuries before Christ.

Jonah likewise is a book which teaches that God was inter-
ested in non-Jews. The Assyrians were also his people despite
their cruel record in relationship to the Jews. While there is little evidence that Nineveh was ever converted, there was confidence that such conversion would please God whether it pleased
his people or not.

Ecclesiastes, or Koheleth, is widely recognized literarily as a
late book of wisdom, written around 200 B.C. It has doubtless
been touched lightly by the spirit of cynicism and otherwise
affected by the Greek spirit. The cyclic view of events reflected in this work was out of keeping with the broader biblical idea that God is always making things new. The promise of
progress and transformation is lacking. There is no hope of life
after death so far as this piece goes nor is there any feeling or
sense of meaning in the cycle of experience.

The book of Daniel provides a source of direct insight into
the era in question, being addressed to the Maccabean period,
especially 168-165 B.C. Like parts of Zechariah, it is apocalyptic
in style and promises transformation of the kingdoms of this
world into the Kingdom of God. The book, as it now stands,
was written to encourage the Jewish people in deep trouble, by
assuring them that their way of life was right. It also raised
the level of future expectation and hope above the historical

scene and promised a general resurrection, not a dead end in Sheol.

However, the canon of the Old Testament was widely accepted by the beginning of the second century B.C. Admittedly, actual canonization did not occur until the time of Jamnia in the early Christian era. For that matter, some of the writings included in the canon were not popularly accepted as early as 200 B.C., but most of the Old Testament affected and influenced the creative era which is our concern in this book.

Apocrypha

The Old Testament Apocrypha consists of either fourteen or fifteen books, according to whether the Letter of Jeremiah is taken as part of the book of Baruch. "Apocrypha" comes from the Greek word *apocryphon*, meaning "hidden," referring to the fact that these books were hidden from common usage either because they were too profound or because they were too dangerously heretical. Be that as it may, they were neither given the authority nor accorded the circulation due canonical books of the Old Testament. The Roman Catholic Church considers the books to be of secondary value (deutero-canonical), but modern Protestant churches do not accord them any real authority, even though Luther and others found them to be of some basic inspirational value.[2]

Old Testament Apocrypha includes the following works:

    1 and 2 Esdras
    Tobit
    Judith
    Additions to Esther
    The Wisdom of Solomon
    Ecclesiasticus
    Baruch
    The Letter of Jeremiah
    The Prayer of Azariah and the Song of the
        Three Young Men
    Susanna

Bel and the Dragon
The Prayer of Manasseh
1 and 2 Maccabees

The first book of Esdras is actually paralleled by the texts of canonical Scriptures, with one notable addition. This is true of no other book in the Old Testament Apocrypha. The text parallels 2 Chronicles 35:1–36:23, the entire book of Ezra, and Nehemiah 7:73–8:12. New material in a famous section (1 Esdras 3:1–5:6) relates the story of three guardsmen at a banquet for the king. For the entertainment of royalty they engage in a battle of wits to decide the strongest power in the universe. Speaking in sequence, the first maintains that wine is strongest; the second says the king; and the third feels that woman possesses most power over the affairs of men. Each makes his case before King Darius and his guests, but the third guardsman, none other than Zerubbabel himself, presents an addendum to his speech. He claims in a great peroration, which is a tangent to the subject of woman, that truth is strongest of all. The guests and the king agree that Zerubbabel has won the battle of wits, and his reward is royal agreement to grant any request he makes. Naturally, he asks that the Jews be allowed to return home and that they be given money and supplies to rebuild the Temple. But in this remarkable story, 1 Esdras consists of material already available in the Old Testament.

Second Esdras, in contrast, is a book unlike 1 Esdras in every respect. This work which purports to come from the hand of Ezra is undoubtedly a composite work written by numerous hands over a long period of time. The contents of the book and their order are relatively simple. After a brief introduction there is denunciation of sin followed by a promise of resurrection in chapters 1-2; however, the main section of the book is made up of seven visions which Ezra allegedly saw.

In the first vision Ezra bewails the fate of man and ponders the mystery of evil in a world where God is good. Not only does he feel that this is unfair to the individual, but he also asserts that God has been unfair in the judgment of Israel. Ezra is astonished at how few people will be redeemed and how many will be condemned. Overwhelmed by unanswered questions about good and evil, and not satisfied with traditional answers, the seer is directed to prayer and fasting as he looks to apocalyptic vision for surcease, if not for clear answers.

Three visions promise the end of the age and victory for God and his faithful few. In the first a widow, mourning over her lost son, when reprimanded is herself replaced by a glorious city. Her son was destroyed Zion and the new city was the promised New Jerusalem. The second vision depicts the Roman Empire in the figure of a three-headed, twelve-winged eagle which shall be destroyed in due course. A final vision tells of the son of man (messiah) coming from the sea to win his victory on earth. Following the visions, Ezra is told to make a record of them, to prepare for death and for the end of the age.

These visions are contained in chapters 3-14 at which point the Aramaic version comes to an end. Latin and Greek manuscripts add chapters 15 and 16 which update the apocalyptic visions to the Roman period. The book as a whole is a weird mixture, typical of the times, consisting of theosophical speculation and apocalyptic vision, struggle with reality and clinging to hope.

Tobit is a charming story of a righteous Jew who even in captivity kept all the rules of Jewish cult and life. He was also given to acts of kindness and mercy which were required by Law. After one of these acts of mercy (burying the body of a strangled man), he was blinded by the droppings of sparrows. As a blind man he became dependent upon the income of his wife who was a seamstress. In anguish because of circumstances, he wanted to die. At the same time Sarah his kinswoman, discouraged with her lot, expressed the same death-wish to God. She had had the unhappy experience of having married seven husbands each of whom died before her marriage could be consummated. The tragic situation was remedied, however, when Tobias the son of Tobit captured a game fish, whose liver and heart had wonderful, magic, and therapeutic powers. In fact, it was revealed to Tobias that smoke from burning these fish parts would drive away Asmodeus, the demon who killed Sarah's seven husbands; and further that ointment made from the same parts would cure Tobit's blindness. So the story, which was made to order for good over bad, ended happily. It was written at the beginning of the second century B.C. and had wide readership among the Jewish faithful.

Tobit defines the content of a righteous life in terms of deeds of mercy, acts of worship, and ritual cleanness. But no longer was this enough to ward off evil, since Tobit, like Job, suffered because of righteousness but was redeemed by magic. In this book there is a strange combination of high morality with pure magic. Neither logic nor fixed tradition prevented such bizarre conglomerates during a period of upheaval and creative searching.

Judith is a work which resembles Esther in many respects. But the heroine is not the bride of a king—she is a widow living during a time when Nebuchadnezzar vowed vengeance on all who would not help him with his victory over the Jews. Holofernes, who had command of the Assyrian troops, sent to punish the Jews, reduced Jewish hopes to desperation after a thirty-four-day seige of Bethulia, the city where they were trapped. At this dramatic juncture Judith entered the story and, like some Deborah or Joan of Arc, encouraged the forces of God. Then using all her feminine wiles, she gained entry to the enemy camp. After an extended period of time and some unusual experiences, she returned to the Jewish camp with Holofernes' detached head. Confusion came to the camp of the enemy and victory crowned every Jewish effort. While Judith is like Esther in some respects, the book has a more patent legalistic religious content than Esther. Judith, a widow, keeps all the rules of ritual purity and fulfills the cult requirements under the most difficult circumstances. At the same time she bends or breaks the great moral laws to confound her enemies. Judith is a legalistic and ritualistic model of religious piety who might be classified as "a reactionary Pharisee."

Additions to the book of Esther total some 107 verses not in the biblical text in its presently accepted form. These verses make up six additional sections including: a dream of Mordecai concerning a great war (11:2–12:6); the edict of Artaxerxes against the Jews (13:1-7); prayers of Mordecai and Esther (13:8–14:19); Esther's admission to the king's presence (15:1–16); the decree of Artaxerxes favoring the Jews (16:1-24); and Mordecai's dream explained (10:4-13).

The additions to the book of Esther were written in the Greek text but are not included in the Hebrew text. They were probably attached in order to correct the absence of the mention of God in the book and also to give more detail to the story. These additions picture Esther and Mordecai, not just as patriots integrated in a foreign culture, but as good, pious Jews in the style of Tobit and Judith. Prayer and personal piety play major roles in these addenda to the Esther romance. Apparently there was a spirit moving in the times which made every effort to subject literary works to a legalistic and ritualistic definition of piety.

The next two apocryphal works come under the general category of sapiential or wisdom literature. The Wisdom of Solomon is apocalyptic in style and purpose while Ecclesiasticus consists of a blending of Law and Wisdom. This work, entitled Wisdom of Solomon, extols wisdom's opposite attitude toward good and bad Jews, determining their ultimate destiny (chs. 1-5). Solomon, the alleged writer, then explains what wisdom is and how it may be gained (chs. 6-9). Finally, the basic viewpoint of the writer is fully illustrated from the history of the Israelites, friends of wisdom, and the Egyptians, enemies of wisdom (chs. 10-19). In the latter section there are several digressions, but the main theme is always recovered in due time.

The Wisdom of Solomon sought to unite the Hebrew concept of wisdom with Greek attitudes sometime during the first century B.C. or perhaps early in the Christian era. Wisdom was equated with the power and presence of God among men. This book personified wisdom beyond any personification found in the Proverbs. There is in the work a feeling that wisdom is like the logos of Greek philosophy. Greek and Hebrew thought are blended in this book.

Ecclesiasticus is the only book in the Old Testament Apocrypha whose date and author are specifically known. Jesus the son of Sirach was a teacher who lived in Jerusalem. He published his book in 180 B.C., and in 132 B.C. his grandson had the work translated into Greek. In an age when Aramaic was popular, his book was written in Hebrew, and it became a very widely read treatise on manners and morals. Jesus the son of Sirach identified Wisdom and the Law but his wise sayings were not, in fact, on a par with the Law.

The book is divided into two sections: Volume I consists of chapters 1-23 and Volume II includes chapters 24-50, followed by an appendix usually numbered chapter 51. While the book does not lend itself to complete or exact outline, still there are sections that deal with special areas.[3]

Ecclesiasticus reflects the attitudes, morals, and manners of the cultured and religious Jew just prior to the Maccabean Revolt. Religious heritage, as recorded in the Old Testament, is taken for granted by the author, who concerns himself with practical and theoretical aspects of existence in the light of faith. The son of Sirach apparently believed neither in resurrection nor in immortality, but held that the good life per se is superior to wickedness. This position raised some contradictions concerning the nature of man and creation which are left unsettled.

The Law was a norm for conduct and Wisdom was de facto identified with Law. Good manners and right conduct were the essence of righteousness. Moderation was the hallmark of the good life whether in appetite, mourning, or conversation. Ecclesiasticus ("church book"), a work patterned after the biblical book of Proverbs, is made up mostly of aphorisms and wise sayings along lines described above. A book of this size and variety defies summary in a short space, but the reader can discern some of the flavor of it from these comments.

Baruch is a shorter work (five chapters) purporting to come from Baruch the son of Neraiah, the secretary and companion of Jeremiah. This document itself claims to have been composed during the Babylonian captivity of the Jews. That claim is not to be taken seriously. Its contents are relatively simple: historical introduction (1:1-14); confession of sins, prayer for forgiveness and salvation (1:15-3:8); Israel told to follow Wisdom in Law (3:9-4:4); and words and promises of hope (4:5-5:9). This pseudepigraph, written during the latter part of the immediate pre-Christian era, identifies Yahweh with the universal creator and, like Ecclesiasticus, equates Law and Wisdom. The book is an attempted accommodation to the world in which Jews were living. Yet, being a composite, in other places it exhibits not the ecumenical and tolerant spirit but a haughty chauvinism. Like other works, this one reflects the changing mood of the times.

The so-called Letter of Jeremiah is not, as it purports to be, a letter from Jeremiah but is rather a discourse against idolatry written by an unknown Jew sometime after 300 B.C. A point of departure for the author is Jeremiah 11:10, which became text for extended remarks about the folly of idolatry.

Three books of the Apocrypha—the Prayer of Azariah and the Song of the Three Young Men, Susanna, and Bel and the Dragon—are additions to the biblical book of Daniel. The Song of Azariah is so titled because Azariah was the Hebrew name of Abednego in Daniel 3. It is the poetic prayer and song of Shadrach, Meschach, and Abednego. It is placed between Daniel 3:23 and 3:24 when the three young men were in the fiery furnace, but it adds nothing to the Daniel narrative.

The book of Susanna tells the story of two elders who passionately desired to have sexual relations with a beautiful maiden named Susanna. She refused and called for help when they sought to force her to give in. The elders reported that she, being an evil woman, had tried to seduce them privately. But Daniel came to the rescue of the fair maiden by getting the two elders to give separate and conflicting testimonies about the alleged crime. As a result of Daniel's help the elders were condemned and Susanna was saved from death in her innocence.

Bel and the Dragon recounts how Daniel showed up as imposters the priests of Marduk in Babylonia. The priests left sacrifices before the god to be eaten and after the passing night the food was always gone. But Daniel secretly sprinkled ashes on the floor and next morning the telltale footprints of the priests and their children could be traced in the Temple. True religion prevailed.

The religious value of these three books, while not profound, is apparent. Righteousness is a shield to Susanna and protects her against wickedness. Worship of idols is senseless, not to be compared with true worship, according to the book of Bel and the Dragon. The story of the three young men is a backdrop against which we see that man's chief end is pursuit of truth. Attitudes of the times about the shield of true piety, contempt for idols, and concern for wisdom are manifestly supported by these mystery stories. The Prayer of Manasseh is a beautiful liturgical confession which is erroneously set in the time of Manasseh and based on the incident of the evil king being temporarily taken prisoner to Babylon (2 Chron. 33:10-16). It was written about 400 B.C. and while not from Manasseh's time, it is an outstanding example of a poetic form of Jewish confession.

The last two books of the Apocrypha are 1 Maccabees and 2 Maccabees whose similarity ends with their titles. First Maccabees is an excellent historical source for the period of the Maccabean Revolt leading to the establishment of the Hasmonean dynasty. After a brief introduction dealing with Alexander the Great (1:1-9), the book divides the rest of the history into the following chronological sections: background for and cause of revolt (1:10–2:70); events in the time of Judas Maccabeus (3: 1–9:22); the reign and times of Jonathan (9:23–12:53); and Simon, ruler and high priest (13-16). The flow of events is clearly traced from the uncertain beginnings with Mattathias to the time when Simon secured both secular and sacred power as prince and priest.

Second Maccabees is not a chronicle of plain history but is somewhat embroidered. In the first two chapters two letters to Jews in Egypt are transcribed (1-2); this is followed by a detailed account of the causes of the Maccabean Revolt including manipulation of the high priesthood and attempted hellenizing of the populace (3-7). The Maccabean Revolt itself is chronicled in 8:1–10:9 and the exploits of Judas Maccabeus are detailed in

10:10–15:36. An epilogue concludes the book (15:37-39). The whole work was written probably just prior to the Christian era.

The Apocrypha, therefore, is a variety of literary source materials from which we draw folklore, poetry, liturgy, history, and social customs. It is sometimes trite as in Tobit, sometimes proper as in Ecclesiasticus, and sometimes most entertaining as in Susanna or Bel and the Dragon.

Pseudepigrapha

Some literature before and in the early stages of the Christian era took the form of pseudepigraphical works. These works are usually legalistic or apocalyptic in style. In each case the book in question claims to have been written by a notable figure who received special direction of God. The Law is read back into the past, and the future is generally seen in supermundane terms. Demonology and angelology are highly developed in the thought patterns of this material; seven archangels and seven archdemons are named. The pseudepigraphical works of the last two centuries before Christ are a bridge between the Testaments that had a considerable influence on the shaping of the patterns of New Testament thought.

Out of a tremendous amount of literature we note those works which are best known in the period just before the Christian era. The following list claims neither to be complete nor to be exhaustive but represents the best known works from two centuries before Christ:

The Book of Jubilees
The Letter of Aristeas
The Book of Enoch
The Testaments of the Twelve Patriarchs
The Sibylline Oracles
The Assumption of Moses
The Psalms of Solomon
The Fragments of a Zadokite Work

There is other extensive pseudepigraphical material, but this list is representative and complete enough to give us insight into the thoughts and feelings of the era.

Generally the works listed above fit into the chronological era which is our primary interest in this volume. Suffice it to say, however, that there was no recognition at the time of the terms "A.D." and "B.C." Since the central event from which we now trace time, the birth of Jesus Christ, had not yet occurred, other pseudepigraphical works continued to be produced in the Christian era. In fact, some of those first composed before Christ are definitely affected and influenced by Christian editors (e.g., Testaments of the Twelve Patriarchs and Enoch).

Jubilees is a commentary and expansion of Genesis. In fact the author, probably a Pharisee living in the time of John Hyrcanus (135-104 B.C.), rewrote the history of the patriarchs in strict accordance with the Law. The patriarchs are depicted as those who kept the letter of the Law and celebrated all the feasts of cult religion.

The book is entitled Jubilees because history is divided into Jubilee periods of forty-nine years, and it follows closely the accounts as given in Genesis 1:1—Exodus 14:31. As is the case with every pseudepigraphic work, Jubilees is said to be God's revelation to some notable figure. In this case Moses is said to have had the vision and was given the instruction from God. All history is recast to support the Law and to claim that the Law had moorings that reached as far back as creation.

The book exhibits an optimistic mood based on the expectation of the messianic era on the earth. It also has a highly developed angelology and demonology. This work combines the idea of supremacy of the Law with apocalyptic vision.

The Letter of Aristeas claims to be a record of the situation under Ptolemy II, Philadelphus (285-247 B.C.), when the Septuagint was written. Actually it is a Jewish apologetic work probably written between 130 and 70 B.C. but rewritten in present form in the first century A.D.

Enoch is the book which has greater direct influence on the intertestamental period and on the early New Testament era than any other of the group now under discussion. It contains a treasure of doctrinal material and answers many of the questions one must raise about this period in the history of Jewish thought.

The book, which must be recognized as having composite authorship, consists of several sections.[4] It deals almost exclusively with the supermundane world where God rules and where demons and angels are always in evidence. The expectation of the end of the age and the coming of the son of man are paramount concepts in Enoch.

Enoch visits the regions of God and reveals the secrets of his journey. He explains evil as having arisen from the joining of the sons of God with the daughters of men. He also tells history's story in ten weeks of time, representing ten ages. By the time this work was finished, apocalyptic style was far advanced and theological ideas were definitely in flux.

The Testaments of the Twelve Patriarchs is a literary piece based on the last words of the sons of Jacob. Each confesses his greatest sin and warns against entanglement of his posterity in the same sin. Virtue was taught through warning and example. Joseph and Issachar are the only sons who can exhibit pure virtue without taint. This book, with some Christian interpolations in the present form of the work, was probably originally written around 100 B.C. It promises a messiah, a descendent of Levi and Judah, and describes Beliar (Belial) as a personal demon almost the negative equivalent of a positive God. However, Beliar even at this stage is destined for destruction after which risen saints will rest in a New Jerusalem, apparently on earth.

The Sibylline Oracles and the Assumption of Moses are also sources but not of primary importance to our study. The Psalms of Solomon is a book of psalms allegedly written by Solomon but actually composed about the middle of the first century B.C.

Fragments of a Zadokite Work, the so-called Damascus Documents, were discovered in a Cairo genizah in 1910. This work concerns a sect of the New Covenant which was founded by a Teacher of Righteousness and which expected the messiahs of Aaron and Israel to come and establish the Kingdom. The group founded by the unique teacher is regulated by the book

of Hagu and is attached in some way to Damascus. Copies of
this work have been found at Qumran among the Dead Sea
Scrolls and a definite connection between the sect of Qumran
and the sons of Zadok in the Zadokite fragment can be made.[5]

The Pseudepigrapha is a vast, amorphous literature, difficult
to date and sometimes hard to assess. Yet from this inchoate
source we are able to reconstruct in some measure the thoughts
and behavior patterns of the time. In these books the attitude of
faith and the shape of life are revealed in general.

The Dead Sea Scrolls

One hardly knows what to say about the fabulous cache of
manuscripts that has come and continues to come from the
Dead Sea area around Khirbet Qumran. For almost two centuries (125 B.C.—A.D. 68) except for an interruption of occupation
from 31 B.C.—A.D. 6, the Qumran plateau was occupied by a sect
of Essenes. These religionists developed a community center
around which daily life and worship were organized and from
which great hopes arose.[6] We shall have more to say about the
Essene sectarian movement.

All texts of the Old Testament, except the book of Esther,
have been found among the manuscripts at Qumran. Other texts
include commentaries on such books as Habbakuk, Nahum, and
Genesis. The commentary in the case of prophetic books makes
the prophecy contemporaneous or at least finds its meaning and
fulfillment in current events of the day.

More important for our purposes in this book are three
scrolls found among the original seven scrolls. They are the
Manual of Discipline, the Psalms, and the War of the Sons of
Light and the Sons of Darkness. The Manual of Discipline describes the discipline and defines the doctrine of the sect.[7] The
Manual provides excellent insight into the doctrine of this particular sectarian group and also gives a more general backdrop
for the times.

In like manner the War Scroll describes the liturgical and
military order for the holy war at the end of time when the

Essenes would fight in the last battle. Psalms also gives considerable insight into the deepest feelings of the worshiper at the time.

The whole Dead Sea literature, involving hundreds of documents, has done much to enlighten an otherwise vague period. These records from the Old Testament, Apocrypha, Pseudepigrapha, and Dead Sea Scrolls, together with other sources from the surrounding world and later writers such as Josephus and Philo are the documents on which we draw. The variety and manifold nature of this literary material underline the fact that this was an era of rapid change both internally and externally. Persian influence mingled with Greek ideas and these encountered the Hebrew faith. The result was a clash and resistance followed by adaptation. This was the creative era when the Hebrew spirit was sorely tested but proved itself adaptable enough to survive. This creative era was a formative period which developed an excellent foundation and atmosphere for the future Christian faith and church.

III

PARTIES AND ATTITUDES

During the Old Testament period, parties within the Jewish nation did not exist. To be sure, there were tensions and differences, but these were never solidified into organized, identifiable religious parties.

The Jewish people had a sense of national and racial unity as long as they lived together in the land of Palestine, but the Babylonian Exile disrupted that togetherness. A resultant diversity of attitude began to manifest itself among the people. This did not become a matter of party strife prior to the Maccabean Revolt. The crucible beginning with the Maccabean period caused the Jews to take different attitudes both toward the world that surrounded them and toward the hope that supported them. When Antiochus IV, Epiphanes, ordered the end of Jewish religion in 168 B.C., the time to react had come. How should this challenge be met? How did it fit into the whole future purpose of God? On the different answers to these questions, different parties started to take shape.

Hasidim

The Hasidim ("pious ones") were not a formal party but a group of devout religious Jews who believed in complete compliance with the requirements of the Law.[1] In defense of that Law they were quite willing to lay down their lives. On one occasion rather than break the Sabbath day many of these extremely conservative Jews allowed themselves to be slaughtered. Early in the Maccabean Revolt the forces of the king came out against an encampment of Jews on the Sabbath. In mortal peril they decided: "Let us all die in our innocence; heaven and earth testify for us that you are killing us unjustly" (1 Mac. 2:37). The Syrians proceeded to slaughter a thousand Jews on the spot; no pious Jew resisted. This event created a crisis in the thinking of Mattathias and his followers who realized that such a policy could lead to Jewish extinction. Therefore, it was decided that Jews would defend themselves when attacked on the Sabbath. The accommodation of the Maccabees to the real situation must have put a strain on relationships with the Hasidim.

Whether the break within the Hasidim movement came during the time of Judas Maccabeus or later is almost impossible to determine. In all probability the Hasidim were satisfied when the Temple was restored and when sacrifice was made. Judas' further military exploits were pressed without support of this conservative attitude.[2]

There can be no doubt that the Hasidim generally ceased to support the Hasmoneans when Jonathan became both priest and prince. They were opposed to the aristocratic priestly party. One can also imagine their horror when Jonathan became at once an ally and an officer in the hated Syrian political structure. The Hasidim who were separatists must have completely withdrawn support by the time of Jonathan. However, the Hasidim represent more an attitude than a party. The attitude changed and parties emerged with varied and differentiated viewpoints out of this original amorphous movement. Indeed both the Pharisees and the Essenes are offshoots of the early Hasidic point of view, while the Zealots are a continuation of belligerent response to foreign intrusion into faith and life. We, therefore, next turn to the parties of thought or to the "four philosophies" of the Jews in the first century A.D., mentioned by Josephus.

Pharisees

The word "Pharisee" is derived from a Hebrew word *parash* meaning "to be separated." This best known of Jewish parties was concerned primarily with the Law, its interpretation, and its fulfillment among the people. They continued the same earnest support of the Law which characterized the Hasidim but were

more willing to accommodate to the situation in time. Most
Pharisees became pacifists and quietists who gave up the idea
of revolt as being completely futile. Their main duties could be
fulfilled in the existent situation.

Pharisees expanded both Law and doctrine to include not
just written material, but also the great mass of oral tradition
which was in process of composition. Scribes, who interpreted
and expanded the Law to meet circumstances, were mainly
Pharisees and successors to Ezra in spirit if not in fact. By creating a "fence of the Law" around the faithful the Pharisees believed that they could remain in the world without being of
the world. Their distinctive life was to be experienced and expressed in the keeping of the Law which set them apart from all
other people. They lived in a world set apart by faith, not in a
world of literal separation.

It was also Pharisees who helped develop new doctrines
and introduce new ideas into the literature and thinking of the
times. Religion was not static nor was Law fixed. Therefore,
these brilliant proto-rationalists were free to think through the
problems of faith and come up with some real answers. Pharisees held a doctrine of resurrection from the dead which went
well beyond the Old Testament concept of Sheol as a neutral
place of rest and waiting. In the resurrection there was to be
both reward and punishment.

The Pharisees also held to a strict view of God's control
over history and the life of man. There was little room for
man's freedom or decision. Beyond the world of sight they saw
the air or atmosphere filled with demons and angels. Like other
Jews they expected a restoration of the kingdom on this earth
in which the dead would be raised up and in which they too
would live.[3]

While the Pharisees were careful to protect themselves against
intrusions and influences of the world, they were willing to
bring their own influence to bear on the world about them.
They were ready to proselyte others into the faith and were
possibly responsible for bringing the Idumeans into Judaism by
force. However, it was in the political field that the Pharisees

made their power felt as early as the reign of John Hyrcanus whose right to the high priesthood they questioned.

Pharisees continued their harassment until, during the reign of Alexander Janneus, the king was temporarily overthrown and exiled by their efforts. The Pharisaic leader Simon ben Shatoh established an interim government while the king was in exile.

Josephus reported that Alexander Janneus, who took vengeance on the Pharisees, later advised his wife to make peace with them. Be that as it may, when Alexandra became queen, she established good relations with the Pharisees and they became a power-force among the people.

This party believed itself to be the true Israel because of adherence to the Law. Defense of the Law by non-violent action and by fulfillment of its precepts became for them a way of life. By building a fence of the Law they were protected from corruption of Gentile influence and by study and interpretation of the Law they were guided into the path of God's will. It was doubtless this emphasis on the study of the Law that created the synagogue as a central institution of Judaism.

Sadducees

The Sadducean party also emerged out of the Maccabean Revolt and in all likelihood derived its name from Zadok who was the father of the legitimate line of Jerusalem priests. Sadducees were composed largely of the upper classes who maintained control of the Temple operation. They apparently supported the Hasmoneans. The Sadducees pre-empted to themselves the office of high priest, since the old Aaronic line had been disrupted during the period under Antiochus IV, Epiphanes, when the priesthood could be bought and sold with great ease.

Sadducees supported the priestly claims of Simon and his successors and kept general charge of the Temple and its priests. Since all doctrine must arise from a strict interpretation of the written Law without expansions, the Sadducees denied resurrection as well as the existence of angels and demons. In theology they held that man was a free agent and not bound or determined by the will of God. These doctrinal denials and this affirmation became the major bones of contention between this party and the Pharisees.[4]

With the rise of the Pharisees to new favor during the reign of Alexandra, the Sadducees were correspondingly on the decline. Still they continued to run the Temple while Pharisees intent on the Law centered much of their activity in synagogues among the people. Often, however, when Pharisees were in trouble with Rome, the Sadducees were able to accommodate to the situation and still carry out their religious functions. With the destruction of the Temple in A.D. 70, Sadducean influence was wiped out and future development of Judaism rested almost entirely in the hands of the Pharisees.

Essenes

One of the four philosophies of the Jews in the first century mentioned by Josephus was the Essene party.[5] Except for references in Josephus and Philo, students knew very little about the Essenes from contemporary sources. That lack was partially filled when the Zadokite Fragment was discovered, but even in that case there was no way to determine whether or not the Zadokites were actually Essenes.[6] Fortunately, material from Khirbet Qumran (the Dead Sea Scrolls) has provided valuable insight into the life and faith of an Essene or Essene-like community.

Unlike the Pharisees, the Essenes decided to remove themselves from contact with society, and, unlike the Sadducees, they were not primarily concerned with Temple sacrifice. The community at Qumran from 125 B.C. until its destruction in A.D. 68 by the Romans was made up of devout Jews who had gone back to the wilderness to meet God in the same kind of setting where Yahweh had met his people and had instructed and led them during the Exodus. A settlement was made in the desert away from the traffic of human society and apart from the corrupting influences of non-Essenes.

In literal response to the prophecy of Second Isaiah these

sectarians had come to the desert to erect the perfect Law community. The passage on which they based both present action and future hope was:

> "In the wilderness prepare the way of the LORD,
>> make straight in the desert a highway for our God.
> Every valley shall be lifted up,
>> and every mountain and hill be made low;
> the uneven ground shall become level,
>> and the rough places a plain.
> And the glory of the LORD shall be revealed,
>> and all flesh shall see it together,
>> for the mouth of the LORD has spoken" (Isa. 40:3-5).

Their preparations for the messianic advent were spiritualized in interpretation, so that building a community utterly devoted to the Law and given to love among its members would assure the coming of the messiah. These were the rough places which needed to be made plain and the crooked which had to be made straight.

Apparently life at Qumran did not go well for some twenty years until a Teacher of Righteousness came to guide the community in its development. Like some second Moses he led the community to a deeper understanding of the Law; salvation, in fact, came by faith according to the teachings of the Teacher of Righteousness and his interpretation of the Scriptures. The Teacher of Righteousness, who cannot be identified (though many have tried), was subjected to persecution if not martyrdom, possibly during the reign of Alexander Janneus. However, there is no basis for the assertion that he was crucified or that he arose from the dead or that he promised to return to his disciples at the end time. That the Teacher of Righteousness was a notable prophetic figure who was critical of religious authorities cannot be denied, but that he was the original of which Jesus was a pale copy can be denied.

Under the direction of this charismatic leader the Qumran community, which was almost certainly a celibate group, waited in hope for the coming messiah and for the new Israel. While they waited, these pious men dwelling in the desert busied themselves with many things, the most important of which was copying and reading the Law. Their greatest treasure was the Law of God which was given into their care and keeping. At least during some periods of time when the plateau was occupied, the members of the community continually meditated or read aloud portions of the Law, fulfilling literally the injunction to meditate on the Law "day and night" (Joshua 1:8).

Essenes were like the Pharisees in their willingness to expand the Law by interpretation, but they were more restrictive in their understanding of its meaning and application. The Sabbath was a day for absolute rest with hardly an exception. Should an animal fall in a ditch on the Sabbath he had to remain there until the end of the Sabbath. In addition to restrictive interpretations, there were many rules and oaths of the community itself to which the members were subject. Failure to comply with certain forms of etiquette and behavior brought temporary or permanent banishment from the center, a punishment which in the desert meant almost certain death.

Entrance into membership in this society of the withdrawn was neither simple nor easy. There was at least one year of probation before the novitiate could become a provisional member. Provisional membership gave him the privilege of participation in the daily sacred bath. Upon passing stiff examinations, swearing oaths, and receiving the vote of the community, he was admitted to full membership, but only after one additional year of probation. In the course of doing all this he had to divest himself of all property and agree to give it to the commonwealth of all. Moreover, he swore to love the brotherhood and to hate all outsiders.

The community was led by twelve elders and three priests. These twelve elders were symbolic in the structure of the new Israel which the Essenes at Qumran considered themselves to be. They were the "righteous remnant" around which God would build his new Kingdom on earth. There was an "overseer" (bishop) for the whole life of the community, but there appears to have been considerable democracy in the rule of the community itself.

Daily activities at the center were generally scheduled around the coming and going of the light. At dawn the Essenes arose from their places of rest (probably booths on the plain or caves in one of the cliffs) and prayed toward the light of the rising sun. This was not because they worshiped the sun, but rather because they considered God the source of light. As suggested above, the conflict of light and darkness was highly developed in the thought of these sectarians who held that God created forces of light and darkness, good and evil, which were to be in perpetual enmity on the plane of history. All men were assigned by God to be sons of darkness or sons of light with little if any choice in the matter. Tension was the texture of life. Struggle was seen in the interplay of light and darkness.

The faithful Essene at Qumran rose at dawn and prayed, then he went to his assigned task. About an hour before noon he came back to the community center which measured 108 feet by 94 feet at the most developed stage and took a sacred bath together with his fellows. For this purpose the center was honeycombed with cisterns and aqueducts, some of which had processional-like steps leading into them. Rules of the Essene community forbade that any faithful member enter water not sufficient to cover his body, indicating that total immersion was required for reasons that escape us. When the sacred bath was over, the full-fledged member was ready for his sacred community meal.

That meal was served in a dining room some 70 feet long where all the full-fledged community members sat to eat together. At the appointed time the priest in charge blessed and broke bread for distribution. This was followed by the passing of the cup to those at the table. The community meal reminded these Essene sectarians of their unity and interdependence as any community meal does. But more, it was rehearsal and preparation for the feast which would mark the coming of the messiah.

These two daily events at Qumran do have formal affinities

with baptism and the Lord's Supper, but the similarities largely end with the form. Baptism for Jews was a new idea showing that all Jews were not considered the people of God by virtue of birth. Not until they affirmed this loyalty by statement of faith was it true. Nonetheless this baptismal rite was not an initiatory rite, but was more a symbolic act done probably in connection with the daily expression of penance.[7]

When evening came, prayer and meditation on the Scriptures continued through the course of the night. Members of this well-organized community of desert holy men knew why they had come to this place and what they expected of the future. Their present life was built around the Law and their future was set within the framework of the coming messiah or messiahs, who would establish them as the new Israel in the land.

Essenes continued to copy their Scriptures and live in strict adherence to the Law. They accepted the tension and struggle of living and history as part of God's created order. This condition would remain until the end time when the darkness was to be overcome and evil put down.

Meanwhile, temptation took the form of attacks of evil on good, the insinuation of darkness into light. Resistance to temptation was assured only in the keeping of the Law.

The messiahs of Israel and Aaron were expected to consummate the Kingdom almost immediately. Meanwhile, in the last days, the little band of not more than 200 men went its way and did its duty in the confidence of faith in an all-powerful God.

Actually there were other Essene enclaves than the one at Qumran, but we have in hand more information about that one than about all the others. Essenes lived generally on the outskirts of civilization, but some groups doubtless had more contact with the outside world than Qumran residents did. Some Essene groups practiced marriage and engaged in other habits not in vogue at Qumran. Since the period during which the Qumran community flourished stretches over most of two centuries, it is not unlikely that there were changes in both form and practice within that one enclave, to say nothing of the differences which would develop between separated and divided groups.

In summary, the Essenes were religious men who withdrew from contact with society and lived in exclusive communities of brotherhood and love for each other. Like the Pharisees they were concerned with the preservation and fulfillment of the Law. Living under the Law and in communion with God and each other, they looked for the almost immediate establishment of the new Israel with the coming of God's messiah. That event would mark the end of darkness and the victory of light.

Zealots

It was only at the beginning of the Christian era that the Zealots as a party among the Jews began to be identifiable. Under the leadership of Judas the Galilean, in the early years of the Christian era, the smoldering flames of revolt again broke out in full fury.

Zealots were the inheritors of the Maccabean spirit of revolt against heathen oppressors. Two attitudes mark the Zealot and set him apart. He was zealous for the Law of God and was ready to die in defense of the Law or in fighting against the enemies of the Law of God.[8]

Zealots, unlike the Pharisees, were willing to fight against the evil, not to co-exist with it. Essenes, unlike Zealots, desired to run away from encounter with evil; Essenes put off their involvement in the battle against evil to the final battle when God himself would dispel the dark forces of evil.

Zealots were Maccabees in spirit two centuries after the Maccabean Revolt.[9] They maintained vigorous opposition to existing political powers and felt that opposition, military or subversive, was in the service of God. Moreover, the Almighty would protect and fight for those that fought for him.

This spirit of revolt finally led to the destruction of Jerusalem in A.D. 70 and its decimation in A.D. 135 at the end of the Bar Cochba uprising. Fighting against Rome was not a very satisfactory approach to the problem, nor was political independence to be part of future expectations for the Jews. The Zealots were revolutionary religious extremists.

Summary

These parties and others such as the Samaritans grew, developed, and interacted upon each other. But not every person was identified with one or another of the factions mentioned. To be sure, there were gradations of difference between Pharisees and Essenes. Exactly when they became separate is all but impossible to say. Some Zealots were almost certainly Pharisees in their faith; only the Zealots were activistic Pharisees, and the Essenes were quiescent Zealots. In all probability War of the Sons of Light and the Sons of Darkness originated from a Zealot but was taken over by the Essenes.[10]

The interplay of groups and ideas remained characteristic of the era which was never really static but always in process. Clashes between parties and the encounter of new ideas against old ideas supply an important part of the creative dynamics of the intertestamental period.

IV
CREATIVE
RELIGIOUS ATMOSPHERE

Change and Movement

The overall impression created by the intertestamental period is one of change and movement. Nothing appears to be fixed, either in patterns of culture or systems of ideas. Held in tension with a strange openness to new ideas was a defensiveness against being forced to accept new attitudes. History and thought were in a plastic state ready to be molded or remolded into yet undetermined shapes.

That change was let loose when the Jewish nation was sent into exile by Nebuchadnezzar in 587 B.C. The Temple was gone and the land was under the heel of a conqueror. Of even greater importance was the fact that the Jewish people were dispersed into foreign lands and were exposed to strange cultures. They resisted the most vigorous challenges, but ideas tend to seep through the dike of opposition to change. The ferment could not be stopped; a new situation in the world and a new approach to life were being fashioned.

The Neo-Babylonian Empire was actually somewhat like an interim between the Assyrian monolith and the Medo-Persian kingdom. With the rise of Persia under Cyrus the Great, an old policy of Assyria was finally canceled, leaving the Jews free to practice their religion and to return home to Judah and Jerusalem if they wished.

Returning to Jerusalem, the Jewish people doubtless expected to take up where they left off. But circumstances had radically changed. For example, they were not a free people, even though their first two governors (Sheshbazzar and Zerubbabel) were from their own ranks. Zerubbabel was deposed in the administrative reform of Darius I, and after that, the Jews, like all other non-Persians, were under a royal satrap or governor from Persia. Judah was but a small part of the vast Persian Empire; her future was bound within the framework of that dominant fact of life.

Jews in the Persian imperial system were free to worship as they had before and they did succeed in restoring the Temple. But those who returned had gone through the ferment of change which had not reached a stopping point. God was no longer the God of a nation alone; he was Lord of heaven and earth—the mighty God above all gods. His final dwelling was not in a place of man's making—he was exalted above every human vision or effort.

How did one please this God who had judged and saved or punished his people Israel? God would be pleased by their keeping of his Law, by their offering of sacrifices of worship in his Temple, and by their following of Wisdom. Prophetic vitality was replaced by scribal legalism in the life of the people. The distinctive purpose of the faithful was to keep the Law to the last letter of exact interpretation and oral expansion. God's Law and purpose were both fixed; nothing new could be expected. Yet much newness did invade faith and life under the guise of explanation and application.

God's Law was to be fulfilled in everyday life as a practical procedure. From earliest time, justice and righteousness were acted out not at a cult center but in the flow of ordinary life. It was only one intellectual step to the production of practical wisdom for the good life. Confusion arose almost immediately between practical wisdom and the Law of God. In due time wisdom was personified and given a place of equal standing with the Law in the devotion of the faithful.

The influence of Persian religion (Zoroastrianism) also made itself felt on the Jews who were cast out of their own accustomed habitat and milieu during the Exile. The individual sometimes had to stand apart from the community and think things out for himself. Since the destiny of the nation was in such jeopardy, what hope was there for him? Life had to be seen in terms of light and darkness in conflict; man had an individual choice. The old forms of corporate life were shattered. But man by choice or destiny could become part of the new community that already appeared on the horizon of hope.

Urgent questions concerning suffering and death were raised. Why did God allow man to suffer? How was the unseen world arranged to make this possible? Such questions could not be silenced because the doctrines of the past were not complete enough to meet the needs of the present. Since many questions went unanswered in life and many inequities seemed unbalanced, it was believed that man should expect a balance in some life after death. That life would be continued as reward for the righteous and as punishment for the wicked—a neutral continuance was no longer acceptable. The judgment of God in history was to be supplemented by the judgment day beyond history, after which the final divine dispositions were to be made.

Persia faded before the power of Greece when Alexander attacked, but the residue of Persian influence remained in the backwash of the empire. Greeks, no longer divided into city-states, underlined the imperial mood and supported a new individualistic approach to life. God to them was the God of the inhabited world and there was but one world. He was exalted above man because he was pure spirit. Man, on the other hand, was a soul encased in a body of flesh which was evil. Hence, man survived, if he survived at all, in a pure spiritual world. Old gods of Greece were cast aside as relics from an ancient time when men deified and worshiped heavenly bodies, dead heroes, and natural forces.

Jewish men of faith began to think in terms of the world of body and spirit, compromising the old concept of the unity of person so long held by their forefathers. They, like the Greeks, saw God far beyond the realm and reach of man and began to believe in angels who were mediators between God and man. These angels had their counterparts in demons.

While Greek thought had lasting influence on the faith of the Jews, it seemed always to solidify the Hebrew attachment to Law and to the worship of Yahweh. While there were always some people ready to make accommodations immediately, most wished to keep the distinctive marks of Law, Temple, and circumcision. After the Greek period ended, the Jews were still a people of the Law who worshiped Yahweh, a God who could not be mistaken for Zeus in whatever form.

New Thought in the Making

Out of this two-century maelstrom, new thought forms were forced to emerge and to take shape. These forms were largely concerned with the unseen world and with future hope. To be sure, the gateway to that unseen world and the ground for hope were matters of extensive discussion in Law, in Wisdom, and in Temple practice. The Law kept had power to fend off the evil forces which beset man in his earthly pilgrimage and such fidelity also identified him as one of the pious in the community of God's people. In addition, wisdom was common sense; proper living in the present assured living hereafter.

Of most significance in this period of process was the fragmentation of man's conception of the unseen world. What had been implicit became quite explicit during this time. This result stemmed in large measure from dealing with the problems of evil and of individual worth. God could not be the source of evil if God were wholly good and righteous.

Where then did evil arise? Not with God! Or if with God, it was evil only with temporal scope and limited power.

The resultant doctrinal structure led to a division between the power of God as the source of all good, and the power of Satan as the epitome of evil. Satan, Beliar, or Azazel became the counterpart of God, and the Jewish faith flirted momentarily with pure dualism. At the same time God seemed to become more and more withdrawn from the world of man; therefore, intermediaries between man and God became a necessity for contact between the two. In Jewish belief, angels in great numbers began to occupy the ether. Seven archangels were balanced off by seven spirits of evil. The world beyond man's experience, the dim unknown upon which man's present well-being and future were dependent, was a divided world in perpetual conflict. The Old Testament concept of struggle between chaos and order gave way to a definite and significant fracture.

Exactly how and when some of these steps in thought came into the intellectual forms of the Jews is not possible to say either with exactness or with confidence. Man's future began to be thought of more in individual terms after the Exile; before that, future hope had been expressed largely in terms of community and people. Community had been disrupted, and man, after the return from Exile, was called upon as an individual to keep the Law and to fulfill righteousness. The true people of God were the faithful ones who kept the Law, not all the Jewish people chosen by some ancient covenant or related to a patriarchal ancestor. Religious faith became a way to assure membership in that invisible community which was made up of God's true people.

Since hope no longer rested on the society or the people of Israel, as such, what was the future of those individuals who died in the faith? Hitherto the line went on from generation to generation in God's chosen nation, but now that nation existed no longer as a political entity. For some there was hope of political restoration and for a time after the Maccabean Revolt it came to pass. But what of those saints of God who had kept the faith but died before hope was fulfilled?

Earlier belief was that all the dead went to Sheol, a kind of storage place for the nebulous shades or souls of the departed. But with the new situation this appeared to be a contradiction of God's promise and power to differentiate in his judgment between the righteous and the wicked. As early as the book of Daniel there appeared a new belief in the resurrection of the righteous to reward, and resurrection of the wicked to punishment. It must be reiterated, however, that the literature is not altogether clear as to whether the later group was destined for eternal punishment or for annihilation.

With the resurrection and reward of the righteous to eternal bliss, the unseen world added one more significant split. Certainly the Jews expected the messiah to come in order to set up an earthly kingdom. In some passages this was conceived of as a return to the paradisal state of Eden and in others it was depicted as a restoration of Israel and Judah to purity and power around Jerusalem. The faithful dead were to be raised up from their graves to participate in that new kingdom on earth over which God's messiah would reign.

Too often, however, the earthly messianic hopes went awry, so men of faith raised their hopes above history. The son of man, coming on clouds of glory, pre-existent from eternity and having dominion over all things, would break through to man. With his coming, the new kingdom would start to be transformed into a spiritual Kingdom of heaven. This resulted from the Greek concept of spirit-flesh division in human nature; only the spiritual element would endure.

Two conflicts in thought patterns had to be resolved in the thinking of the time: first, how to rid the world of evil, and second, how to relate the structures of hope for the future. Early in the growth of a divided universe concept, it became evident that God would limit the power of evil; eventually he would bind Beliar and cast him into the pit of destruction along with all the evil spirits and demons which infested the earth. In fact, the Almighty had immediate power over these creatures at any time and their purposes could be thwarted. The final place of binding Satan and his minions became a kind of embryonic hell.

The messianic kingdom and the Kingdom which was, in fact, a new heaven and a new earth were cleverly juxtaposed. There would be an earthly kingdom, a restored Israel, for a period of time. Into this domain all the righteous living and dead would be brought. Some had been left dead for a season in Sheol which had become an intermediate state. These all would be gathered for a season on earth, then the temporary earthly kingdom would become a spiritual or heavenly Kingdom.

Meanwhile, with these structures of faith and visions of hope as a backdrop, man lived on the earth trying to develop a life of singleness under the Law, guided by wisdom and inspired by cult worship. But his eyes were on the unseen world toward which he moved and to which he aspired.

Understanding of Struggle

This last two hundred years before the coming of Christ was a time of struggle and suffering for the Jewish people. Enoch and others explained that suffering arose from evil spirits which infested the earth; these were the corrupt spirits of fallen angels and their offspring. Suffering was caused by the adversaries who tested and sometimes sought to destroy the powers of men.

Most evil and all sickness could be traced to demons or to evil spirits. Demon possession became a prime superstition, and exorcism took on new importance. Men, bound by Satan, could be set free only by God. This understanding of the nature of the unseen was current when Jesus walked among men. The unseen world of Jesus' disciples and contemporaries was fabricated out of these same materials.

Temptation was understood as the attack of these unseen but real forces of darkness on the lives of the righteous. Faith was a battle, a struggle to beat down the fiery darts of the evil one who lies in wait to trap man. Later language in the New Testament makes real sense in the light of this fact. "And bring us not into temptation, but deliver us from the evil one" (Matt. 6:13, A.S.V.) are not words drawn out of abstract thought. Man was up against the constant attack of evil forces in the world. Temptation was the method of that attack.[1]

The texture of life, therefore, was struggle against "principalities and powers"; there was more to it than strife between flesh and blood. History and life were to be understood as a time of great conflict between good and evil. Men must choose to be, or, according to some thinkers, men were chosen to be, the sons of darkness or the sons of light.

Fortunately the Dead Sea Scrolls have largely cleared up the basis for the struggle. God himself created forces of darkness and light, evil and good, from the beginning. It was he who set them at perpetual enmity against one another; God kept control over the conflict at all times. The triumph of God was never in doubt nor were his faithful in real jeopardy. Yet the struggle was very real and all men were engaged in it at all levels of life and experience.

At the end time, God, who ordained struggle as the testing time for the righteous, would bring the conflict to an end. Evil would be beaten down and good would triumph through the righteous sons of light. The earth would be cleansed of evil and there would be a new heaven and a new earth.

In the final battle, men of righteousness were to join the forces of God in destroying the powers of evil. Plans for such warfare are clearly laid out in War of the Sons of Light and the Sons of Darkness. Meanwhile, the sons of light remained pacifistic because battles this side of the ultimate battle were meaningless. For this reason Pharisees and Essenes saw little cause for supporting the revolutionary program of the Zealots.

While life lasted, it would be a life of struggle against evil; there could be no peace for the sons of light so long as the sons of darkness were abroad. In struggle men learned to depend upon God and through endurance righteousness was wrought in character. Daniel promised that the struggle with Antiochus Epiphanes would end in triumph and it did after three or more years. But evil remained. The promise was projected beyond the present to the end time for those who endured the crisis and remained faithful.

Suffering, as a redemptive process, did not receive much emphasis in this latter period. The idea of the suffering servant was all but forgotten in the time just before Jesus appropriated it for his own use. Suffering was a result of conflict; testing or temptation was to be endured. It purified the sufferer and made a witness to the nations about the faith of those who endured.

Life was in tension and conflict. That was its nature. Only the end of life and history would conclude the conflict; any peace before that day would be abject surrender.

The Need of Man

Sin was, according to the views of the times, rebellion against God, but more, it was a permanent condition of man's life. Actually the period produced the idea of *yetzer*, that sin was to choose the wrong tendency in life. There were for men a good tendency and a bad tendency which were assigned by God or which men were free to choose. To be in opposition to God, whether by choice or by chance, was the essence of sin itself.

Sin originated, according to Jesus the Son of Sirach, with woman who through fornication corrupted the angels of God. The tendency to trace sin back to the fall of man in the Garden is found in 2 Esdras. Further, the corruption of Adam had, according to this document, been passed down through inheritance to all of Adam's progeny. Therefore sin appeared to be an inner bent toward rebellion against God which was present in practically all people.

Sin made itself known in evil speech and in sexual desire, according to the Son of Sirach. But sin to him was a willful and deliberate opposition to the purpose of God. Since this was part of human nature, how could it be cured? Only God could provide cure for the evil that had corrupted human nature.

Forgiveness came through repentance, not through sacrifice or fasting. These acts of penance could well follow the moment of contrition when the sinner became genuinely sorry for his rebellion against God. Motivation of the heart became central to God's forgiveness of the penitent. After repentance there had to follow a new quality of life expressed in almsgiving and in sacrifice.

Sin was a condition of man's life, sometimes traced back to his creation in Adam, but sin was also willful breach of the Law of God in thought and in deed. Further, sin was thought to be the choice of the wrong tendency in man's makeup, if indeed he had a choice. Or in the last analysis, sin was to become a son of darkness rather than a child of light. However expressed, sin had become more than the sum total of sins—it was a condition of man's life. Nor could salvation be wrought by man. Only God could forgive or judge; only he could cure and restore.

Therefore, man's condition required God's direct action. Forgiveness came by God's action, not by man's effort. Even the Jews who were a chosen people were now divided into the redeemed and blessed as over against the judged and condemned. God's people was a new Israel who chose light, not darkness; good, not evil. Yet even with the good, there was failure and the necessity of developing a doctrine of divine forgiveness available to the pious penitent. That need was not met clearly in any of the literature of the times.

Worship in the Synagogue

The plight of the Jews from the time of the Neo-Babylonian Exile onward caused two inevitable institutional developments. These were the synagogue and the school, which though closely connected were not identical. Judaism believed that all its people should be taught the revealed Word of God; to this end the two institutions came into being.

While there is considerable difference of opinion about the origin of the synagogue and little definite evidence to go on, certain lines of emergence can be traced. There can be little doubt that the institution had its inspiration in the Exile where the Jews far from home gathered, probably on the Sabbath, to remember Zion and to recall the Law. Some of Ezekiel's meetings with the exiles at Tel-Abib could be so interpreted, which is not to say that a formally organized synagogue came into being at that early time. However, the need for study and for preservation of the faith did exist in that exilic situation. Out of these needs the synagogue finally came.[2]

By the time of Ezra it is probable that there were further developments with schools where scribes taught the substance of the Law to their students. However, it was the general dispersion of the Jews which brought the synagogue into definite and formal existence. Some center was needed in a foreign land around which Jewish life could be ordered; some way had to be found to teach the Law which had been forgotten and to preserve the faith which was imperiled.

Synagogues outside Palestine were almost certainly in use by the middle of the third century B.C., when the Ptolemies were in control of Palestine. Great synagogues were established in Egypt, where translation of the Torah and other Scriptures into Greek was accomplished for use among Jews who could no longer read or understand Hebrew. Notable among synagogues in the dispersion was one in Alexandria which quickly became a center of Jewish life and culture.[3]

Within Palestine an early form of the synagogue likely had been established by the time of the Maccabean Revolt. Some form of a community center of worship and instruction was necessitated at this time of crisis when the substance of faith was jeopardized by political edict and by the infiltration of foreign ideas. The need to retain those who had gone away from the faith of the fathers required both school and synagogue.

By the beginning of the Christian era the synagogue had a fixed place in the life of the Jewish people both inside and outside of Palestine. The synagogue was a visible edifice in Jewish communities and served as a community center as well as a place of worship. Worship in the synagogue was not like that of the Temple, where sacrifice and liturgy were formal and, as has been aptly described, rational in nature. A regular part of the synagogue service was instruction which became in time the most prominent feature of its worship service. Learning and study were key aspects of any synagogue program which was closely associated with the school. By the time of Jesus and during the ministry of Paul the synagogue was common in Jerusalem and in every locale where a Jewish settlement was found in the Roman Empire.

There were three fixed, or at least common, elements in the synagogue worship—prayer, the reading of Scripture, and, when a teacher was available, a homily. The service began with the traditional "shema" ("Hear, O Israel, the Lord thy God . . .") which was introduced and followed by blessings or ascriptions of praise to God. Toward the end of the first century A.D. there were eighteen or nineteen blessings used before and after the shema; these are called *shemoneh esreh* (eighteen) in Hebrew. Traditional prayers began with benedictions followed by petitions and concluded with ascriptions of praise to God.

Following prayer there was reading of the Scripture in the synagogue service. Probably this began with reading of the Law in connection with festivals, but with the passage of time the Prophets also were read. Reading was for the purpose of instructing the hearer through knowledge of records of revealed religion. It is not germane to this book's purpose to trace further the synagogue Scripture-reading program; suffice it to say, it was designed to include the whole Law in a regular sequence over a limited period of time. Religion was more and more centered around the synagogue, which was well adapted to the need for propagating the faith and preserving the tradition.

Homilies were common in the early Christian era, having become an expected part of the service of worship. Preaching was done mainly by those who were especially trained as teachers or recognized for their knowledge. Sermons were the freest form in the synagogue service and offered a forum for the expression of ideas. Faith was kept relevant to the day and tradition was brought to bear on the lives of people. Usually the sermon was in Hebrew, possibly with translation, while some of the Scriptures were read in the vernacular which gave rise to the translation of the Old Testament into Greek beginning about 250 B.C. Most sermons dealt with two great themes: piety and holiness in service of God, and benevolence and uprightness in relations with men.

The synagogue was the institution which together with the school preserved and vitalized the Jewish faith in a difficult period. Jesus was trained in a synagogue as were most of his disciples. Galilee was more heathen than faithful during the Maccabean period, but thanks in large part to the synagogue, Galilee was made up of religious and faithful Jews when Jesus lived there.[4]

It is obvious that the synagogue together with communities such as the one located at Qumran were prototypes for Christian churches both in worship and order. The rise of the synagogue was one of the most significant institutional developments in this period. Its influence on the emergence of Christianity and the growth of Judaism is immeasurable. To this day, nineteen or twenty centuries later, Jews meet in and build their community around synagogues.

History in Crisis

It is almost trite to say that the world seemed to be waiting for the crowning event or the climactic moment. History had moved with its empires of Persia and Greece to the collision point with Rome, which from uncertain beginnings emerged into a mammoth empire of staggering proportions. For a time Rome interfered as an outsider, influencing though not trying to control events, but causing trouble for those who sought control in the Middle East. Even Pompey's take-over of Judah and Jerusalem in 63 B.C. did not signal the end of the Jewish hope for freedom.

In retrospect, the interlude of Hasmonean rule is almost too much to believe. The Jewish people were politically and spiritually free for almost a century. But that came to an abysmal end through internal dissension and through the brutal pressure of Roman power.

With the dawn of the Augustan Age and the elevation of Herod the Great to absolute power in the region of Palestine and its environs, hope for political freedom faded. Pharisees built their fences of Law very high, using both synagogue and school to instruct the people in the separate life. Scribes busied themselves interpreting the Law of God to meet the needs of their situation in life. Apocalyptists updated prophecy to give it meaning that was current and relevant to the events of their times. Sadducees kept the apparatus of the Temple in motion and the cult operative to fulfill the forms of righteousness.

In the desert, Essenes remained withdrawn from and out of contact with the corrupt world. Their new Israel of faith and brotherly love took the form of an organized community in the wilderness of Judea. Daily in worship they made sacrifice with their lips in praise and worshiped God the source of light from whom the Law had come.

All together looked for the messiah or the messiahs who

would come to establish a kingdom on the earth. For some of the faithful there was uncertainty about whether the kingdom was to be in heaven or on earth. Each devout man had to struggle with the problems of suffering and pain. Varied answers were given concerning the source of evil, but no system of thought proved entirely satisfactory to the earnest inquirer.

There was, however, a general consensus that evil was always under the control of God, who had created it as a subsidiary force or by his sufferance allowed it to operate on the plane of history. Evil would be destroyed by the power of God; Beliar or Satan would be bound in his hell of fire together with his minions. All men would rise from the dead to receive on judgment day their due reward or punishment. Heaven and hell were part of the furniture of man's thinking.

The exact nature of salvation was not clearly worked out in synagogue and Temple. It was both corporate and individual but largely spiritual in nature. The individual soul survived, leaving the unity of personality in question. How man was to be forgiven remained a large question as did the means by which the awesome flaw of sinfulness was to be removed from his nature.

In politics Rome dominated the scene; in religion Pharisees had control of the faith and were its interpreters. The synagogue was a center for learning and worship while the Temple kept its place as the locale for sacrifice and cult practice. Zealots were busy with revolt and Pharisees were active in study. Essenes waited vainly for the long-expected messiah.

The atmosphere was one of upheaval which gave rise to hope in the midst of despair. This was a time of creative change; only the exact form of things to come was still to be determined. The stage was filled with several parties who lived in the same visible world, but who saw the present unseen world and the future hope in different terms. In due course, as we have seen, points of view became parties. This development had already happened when Jesus began his ministry and mission in Palestine.

V
EMERGING
THOUGHT PATTERNS

Wide-ranging shifts of political power occurred in the immediate pre-Christian period. However, these surface changes were minor when compared to the deeper upheaval in thought patterns. Persian ideas invaded the minds of people, creating a dualistic approach to the universe. The Greeks divided reality into the material and the spiritual. Unable to do much to reform external circumstances in which they lived, Jews became adept in changing the forms of faith. This was possible because freedom in thought processes had not yet been restricted by doctrinal pronouncements or by official canonization of Scriptures. Even so, in order to get one's ideas introduced and accepted it was necessary to write under a pseudonym.

One World Culture

Second Isaiah understood the implications of Babylonian captivity for the Jews and spelled out clearly his conclusions through his brilliant poetic oracles. God alone was God and there was no other; the old concept that God was a national God disintegrated under the pressure of captivity. Out of the ashes of despair the God of all creation emerged clear and sure. Actually, the God of Moses' faith was the supreme God, as was Yahweh of the eighth-century prophets, but the full implications of that fact had not been drawn until Second Isaiah's day. One world had but one God. He not only ruled in Israel; he commanded that Babylon be destroyed and claimed Cyrus as his unwitting servant. This God was Yahweh the God of Israel, but all nations were within his domain, also all creation was in his field of power. He who held all creation in the palm of his hand could not be wearied by effort nor could he be captured or imprisoned in any idol fashioned by hand or mind.

The one world under one God was even more firmly established as a fact of life with the rise of Cyrus the Great, who himself took over the kingdoms of the world and made them one. His enlightened religious power was proof in the eyes of the faithful that God did control Cyrus and the affairs of men to the ends of the earth. The Almighty appeared at Belshazzar's feast and brought an end to the hated empire of the Chaldeans (Dan. 5). God moved equally well in his action on the broad stage of history or in pinpointing his effort at Jerusalem around the Temple, which was being built by his command.

Following Cyrus and his successors, Alexander the Great united a more extensive world in his political organization. Moreover, military conquest and imperial politics were implemented by an attitude of life, the Greek way. The Golden Age of Greece had long since passed when Alexander came onto the scene. Empire had brought an end to the city-state with its emphasis on community as seen at its zenith in Plato's works. Instead there was a genuine cosmopolitan flavor to Greek thought together with a seemingly contradictory individualistic approach to life. Many Olympian gods were replaced by the one god Zeus, now newly conceived as god alone over all creation. He ruled over the entire inhabited universe (*oikoumene*), and there was no other. The former gods were understood as heroes deified upon death, or natural forces personified, or heavenly bodies elevated to the status of deity. Actually, there was but one God who was involved in the created world with which man had to make his peace. The world was one and God was one both for the Greek and for the Hebrew. Zeus was the great god of Greek thought and Yahweh was the one god of Hebrew faith. But both could not be God. In one world there was no room for two universal gods.

One thing had happened that could not be changed: the world was no longer quite as fragmented as it had been, nor was it as parochial. The empire overshadowed its diverse sections; small states were swallowed up in the great political structures men created. So also smaller gods became angels or spirits in the new order of things. Moreover, a god so grand in conception required intermediaries between himself and men in the form of angels or of *logoi*. What man of flesh could possibly reach directly the one high and lifted above man in space and in moral perfection?

The concept of a god who is God alone in one world raised some real problems about the origin of evil, the place of sin, and the purpose of history. It was no longer possible to explain evil as conflict between competing gods since petty gods had been demoted, nor was it feasible to accept a naïve view of nature as a process-god. If God stood above all, whence came evil? Since God stood outside nature and had control over it, why then did he not control the harmful and evil forces which were part of nature's flow? These were serious problems and burning questions which the new theology raised.

While external history was unified under one God, the unseen world of faith was divided into different regions. An embryonic dualism began to infiltrate Hebrew faith; before the end of the era, it took definite form. The world of events and history had been united by political and military means but the world of ideas and hope began to be thoroughly fragmented by men's thoughts.

The Unseen World

Most Old Testament literature depicts Yahweh as sovereign over all natural powers and human principalities. He is the Lord of hosts who rules over the armies of stars in the heavens and the military forces of men on the earth. Whether this doctrine began with Moses or with the eighth-century prophets, it reached a clarity of expression, as we have pointed out, in Second Isaiah during the sixth century B.C. God was presented as the source of both good and evil in many sections of the Old Testament. Making God the source of evil appears to have caused little problem in the early Hebrew mind. However, the inclination to see God as the direct source of everything now began to be seriously questioned.

In like manner, the problem of individual life came in for study after the Exile. Ezekiel recognized that "the soul that sins shall die" (cf. Ezek. 18). If this be so what then happens to the righteous who die without fulfillment or peace? There was no hope in death because the dead were merely shades who, after death, were stored away in a kind of "non-existence" in Sheol (later Greek Hades). If the kingdom did not come before the death of the righteous, what then? There was no separation between the righteous and the unrighteous, the good and the bad. The promised kingdom of God in some bright future was located in the earth, not beyond it. And the messiah was expected to come to the place where the Jewish people lived on earth.

Ideas about the form of the unseen world began to change in countless ways; concepts about it were in creative flux. While the external world of men and nations was united, the unseen world was in process of fragmentation. God, according to the new theology, had a counterpart in the form of Beliar. Just as God dwelt in light so Beliar dwelt in darkness. A real division, reminiscent of Zoroastrianism, evolved between the domain of God and the dominion of the evil one.

Some scholars identify this development exclusively with Zoroastrian influence following the division between Ahura Mazda (the good light) and Angra Mainyu (Ahriman, the evil spirit), but this conclusion is probably overdrawn. Whether ancient Zoroastrianism was actually dualistic remains a real problem. In later times the Persians and others increasingly accepted a dualistic partition of the universe. Persian influence was doubtless a relatively small factor in the development of the tendency toward dualism among faithful Jews.

Angels and Demons

This growing system began in some measure with the attempt to explain the testing of men in Job. According to the prologue to Job, which is literarily late, Satan is depicted as the adversary under complete control of God (Job 1–2). Events, not literary efforts, raised serious questions about God's control over the whole unseen world. Sin and evil were factors in human life; whence did they come?

One answer was given in a remarkable passage or section of Enoch, where the "watchers," angels or heavenly beings (the sons of God), were enticed by the daughters of men (cf. Gen. 6:4). Sexual union between watchers and women resulted in the birth of giants (Nephilim) who either corrupted or destroyed mankind. In the flood, these fallen angels and their offspring were destroyed. However, their spirits remained to corrupt and to delude man. Enoch, an anonymous Jew of the period, believed in a world of demons and evil spirits, of God and Satan (cf. Enoch 6–36).

Mastema was the adversary not unlike Satan in Job, according to Jubilees 17:16-18. According to the text of Jubilees, he tested the righteousness of Abraham in connection with the sacrifice of Isaac and was the adversary par excellence in the Moses story (Jubilees 48:1-19). Mastema was the prince of the underworld, like Beelzebul, but his main function was testing men under the limitations set by God. Azazel in Enoch performed the same general functions under a different name. He was prince of the fallen angels; he stood in direct opposition to the will and purpose of God. To confuse the issue more, Beliar appeared in the Testament of the Twelve Patriarchs as the prince of darkness and the antithesis of God himself. Sin entered through the watchers, and corruption remained in the world because the spirits of the watchers under the direction of Beliar remained a force in history. While there was yet no solid form to doctrines about the two worlds, there began to emerge a two-kingdom theory. Men of faith lived in the unified world of history and a fragmented world of vision and hope.

The spirit of Beliar possessed Potiphar's wife and caused her to try to seduce Joseph. In the book of Tobit, Sarah the distant kinswoman of Tobit was widowed seven times before her marriage to Tobias was consummated. Each time her bridegroom died before the wedding night. This became not only bewildering but discouraging to the bride (Tobit 3:7-17). Happily the cause was found to be an evil demon known as Asmodeus. The demon, as it happened, could be exorcized by the smoke from a fire burning the inner part of a fish (Tobit 6:1-17). Asmodeus fled to upper Egypt upon smelling the smoke and was bound there (Tobit 8:4). Sarah and Tobias married without mishap.

Life was infected with and influenced by spirits. Heathen gods were transformed or transmuted into evil spirits. They, together with the angels, were agents who controlled man's life. There was a level of conflict and crisis above and beyond history.

God, in the thought of that time, had been raised far outside the horizons of ordinary life which required intermediaries or messengers. Archangels of God had charge of myriads of unfallen angels who served in and above the world. Archangels grew into definite personalities with names and job descriptions. Several places in the pseudepigraphical writings mention four archangels: Michael, Raphael, Gabriel, and Phanuel (cf. Enoch 9:1; 40:9; 71:8-9). In later passages seven archangels are listed and named: Uriel, Raphael, Raguel, Michael, Saraqael, Gabriel, and Remiel (Enoch 20). Many angels served God and protected the faithful in the earth.

Balancing off these seven archangels, seven spirits of deceit came into being, but these were not given names even though their quality is made evident. They were: spirit of fornication, spirit of insatiableness, spirit of fighting, spirit of obsequiousness, spirit of pride, spirit of lying, and spirit of injustice (Test. of Reuben 3:1-6). Beliar was in charge of all these evil spirits which attack man. In the Testament of Dan the reader is told "And now, fear the Lord, my children, and beware of Satan and his spirits" (Test. of Dan 6:1). Beliar and Satan were here used interchangeably, but one cannot be quite sure that the spirits of deceit are so completely personalized as are the archangels who have names. Sometimes the literature speaks of Satans and at other times of Satan because this was in fact a descriptive noun applied to the adversary or to adversaries as the occasion demanded.

Within the book of Enoch there are twenty-one fallen angels: (1) Samjaza, (2) Artaqifa, (3) Armen, (4) Kokabel, (5) Turael, (6) Rumjal, (7) Danjal, (8) Neqael, (9) Baraqel, (10) Azazel, (11) Armaros, (12) Batarjal, (13) Busasejal, (14) Hananel, (15) Turel, (16) Simapesiel, (17) Jetrel, (18) Tamael, (19) Turel, (20) Rumael, (21) Azazel. Despite the duplication of two names, this is an imposing array of chiefs of fallen angels (Enoch 69:2-3). Small wonder religion had to become almost as concerned with the unseen world as with the real world. As if this were not enough, there was a different list of five Satans who are not the same as the fallen angels. They are Jeqon (inciter), Asbeel (deserter from God), Gadreel, Penemue, and Kasdeja (Enoch 69:4-12). These Satans, under the guidance of Azazel, could, however, be fended off by the four or seven archangels who stood around the throne of the Lord of spirits (Enoch 40:1-10). The struggle went on among the powers of the air, and man was a participant in an essentially cosmic struggle. The two centuries before the advent of Christ were a superstitious age where pure monotheism of an earlier day was shattered by a secondary pluralism of demons and angels. This fact explains the use of demons as the cause of sickness and any other evil that befell men in New Testament times.

Heaven and Hell

Concepts of heaven and hell also grew out of the split-level doctrine of good and evil in conflict. All things were divided into darkness and light, evil and goodness. Ultimately the prince of evil, by whatever name, would be bound as Asmodeus was and cast into a fiery abyss together with all his cohorts and their followers. There the evil would suffer either eternal punishment or annihilation. In the course of life all men became either the sons of light or the sons of darkness. In some places this appears to be a matter of man's choice while at other times man was assigned to one or the other by God (Manual of Discipline). At the end time the righteous would be freed from the bonds of Beliar or Azazel or Satan and would live in Eden and New Jerusalem. Whether these names represent mundane sites constitutes a real puzzle. Renewal of the whole universe went hand in hand with revival of the kingdom of the Jews.

Everlasting life or real resurrection was clearly suggested in only two admittedly late passages of the Old Testament: Isaiah 26:19, composed during the third century B.C., and Daniel 12:2, from the second century B.C. Daniel moved beyond a doctrine of Sheol where there was no division of the just and the unjust (Enoch 22:3-4) to a differentiation of these two elements in humanity. Thus eternal bliss and eternal damnation became extensions of the division between light and darkness. Meanwhile the doctrine of a day when God would judge all men unfolded. As a result Sheol tended to become a storage or intermediate place for departed souls until the day of judgment. Even in this intermediate state the righteous would be blessed and the evil would be in misery.

Conflict and Hope

This light-darkness, good-evil motif was a constant theme in intertestamental thought among the Jews. While it is almost impossible to trace the exact development of these thought patterns in chronological sequence, it is evident that the unseen world became more or less splintered, being inhabited by multitudes of angels and demons. In keeping with the Greek frame of reference, the writer of Jubilees spoke of angels of clouds, darkness, winter, etc. This development was a far cry from the God of all creation who holds direct sway over the farthest reaches of his world. While there was some real confusion in the shifting, changing situation, it was dynamic and creatively moving.

The pattern that developed out of this chaotic upheaval in man's thinking and believing can be most clearly seen in one of the Dead Sea Scrolls, the Manual of Discipline. Speaking of God as Creator, the writer explains the presence of and tension between light and darkness but maintains God's sovereignty over both.

He created man to have dominion over the world and made for him two spirits, that he might walk by them

until the appointed time of his visitation; they are the
spirits of truth and of error. In the abode of light are
the origins of truth, and from the source of darkness
are the origins of error.[1]

The writer explains that it is the angel of darkness who causes
men to stray from the light of God. Whether by choice or
divine assignment, all men serve either the darkness or the
light. There is no neutrality. The works or results are manifest in the quality and character of the two which stand in
opposition both in motive and in result. The manuscript elab-
orates on how this situation came about by saying that God
created these two forces and maintains control over them.
"For God has established the two spirits in equal measure
until the last period, and has put eternal enmity between
their divisions."[2] These forces continue to struggle in the life
of man, according to the Manual, until the end time when
God will tip the balances in favor of light over darkness. At
that moment the sons of light will rise up and join God in
the final conquest of evil.[3] Evil will be destroyed and darkness
will flee before the face of light at the climactic and final
moment of history. Beliar will be bound and all his henchmen
cast into the fiery pit prepared for them. Meanwhile the
struggle and the testing goes on, and man must have the
whole armor of God to stand—to hold out until God inter-
venes.

Many religious groups recognized the real division and
tension in history that is described in the inconsistent terms
given above. Even in life the division must be healed by
singleness of heart and purpose. Issachar, who was depicted as
being quite righteous, commends this quality to his children,
saying, "Keep, therefore, my children, the law of God, And
get singleness . . . " (Test. of Issachar 5:1). This sounds somewhat like Jesus' saying, "No one can serve two masters; for
either he will hate the one and love the other, or he will be
devoted to the one and despise the other. You cannot serve
God and mammon" (Matt. 6:24). Moreover, the writer of the
Testaments of the Twelve Patriarchs says that in the time of

wickedness, "Your sons will forsake singleness" (Test. of Issachar 6:1). This desire for unity, for singleness of life, was becoming an aspiration.

The unseen world was clearly seen and sought, but it was a world in flux; the tremors of history had left crevasses of division. The atmosphere in the New Testament was created and must be understood in these terms; the drama of Christ can be perceived best against this background. Yet all faith was not lifted above the earth into the unseen; the real struggle continued on the earth itself.

Faith and Life

The twin themes of faith worth living by or dying for and the protective care of the Almighty are struck again and again in Daniel.[4] People were told that their faith and their way of life would endure because it was established by God. Far from being out-of-date and irrelevant to life, this faith of the fathers made for good health and profound hope. Other structures of power were sheer madness (Dan. 4); it made better sense to die than to bow down before the dumb idols of men's making (Dan. 3 and 6).[5] These were God's people through whom he was still at work and whom he would preserve if they remained faithful in diet, daily prayer, and refusal to worship idols.

It was, however, one thing to talk about the simple virtues of daily life and quite another to set the whole experience of faith and hope in the broader perspective of world history. Where did God's people belong in the whole blueprint of his plans and purposes?

To these questions of faith the book of Daniel spoke in the visions of the latter part of the work and in chapter 2 which is a combination of vision and story. History of recent times was organized into four empires which succeeded one another upon the earth. These kingdoms were the Babylonian, the Median, the Persian, and the Greek Empires. Similarly the beasts of chapter 7 represented the same four empires in succession, and in chapter 8 the ram and the he-goat referred to the struggle between the Medo-Persian Empire (ram) and Alexander the Great (he-goat). God promised that the kingdoms would be destroyed and the Kingdom of God would fill the earth.

The "son of man," according to Daniel, would come on clouds to rule over the new Kingdom. Later the saints would receive the Kingdom which belongs both to the saints and to the son of man. Whether the son of man was a personification of Israel or a future messiah, God's faithful people would not only be saved but would possess ultimate power (Dan. 7:13-14).[6]

Meanwhile, present evil times of suffering were to last in excess of three years, but the tides of history remained under the control of God.

The Jews of the Maccabean period were at the center of sacred history, not lost among the great empires which God could raise up and destroy with equal dispatch. God's faithful people were heirs to his Kingdom. By their faithfulness and endurance they would inherit the Kingdom which would fill the earth and which would know no end (Dan. 2:35, 44-45).

The Jews, far from having lost their identity, were a distinctive people whose heritage set them apart. They were also distinctive in that they were heirs of God's everlasting Kingdom (Dan. 7:13-22; 8:15-27). There was concern among them with wisdom and with hope, wisdom to live well now and hope in God for the future. They were existentially concerned with survival, that is, survival of their ancient way of life and personal survival in the ultimate scheme of things. Faith guided them in life and lighted the future with hope. Faith for the Jew was a healthy combination of practice and aspiration. Faith showed a man how to live in the present and gave insight into how he would live beyond the present.

Law and Wisdom

The Law of God was generally recognized as the basis for righteous life among the Jews of the era 200 B.C. to A.D.

30. From Ezra onward, Law (Torah) was paramount in the
religious life of the people. Interpreting and teaching the Law
were the primary functions of religious life. By the keeping of
the Law the attacks of Beliar were thwarted and atonement for
sin was made (Ecclesiasticus 3:30).

A novel development in this period of time merged the
Law with popular Wisdom. In fact, Jesus the Son of Sirach
equated wise sayings with the Torah of God. His aphorisms
and good advice on manners were thought to be of equal
importance with the laws of God. In fact, this identification
of Wisdom with Law probably reached its zenith in Ecclesiasticus
(19:20; 21:11; 34:8).

Law emphasized the keeping of the Sabbath as a regular
part of righteousness before God. This was especially true in
the book of Jubilees where the Sabbath is traced back to
the beginning of creation. On the Sabbath all work ceased
by command of God; normal sexual relations between husband and wife were forbidden on the holy day and other
activities stopped. The Sabbath became so important that popular belief held that the Sabbath was kept in heaven by
God and his holy angels.

The Law of God was considered by the faithful to be
universal and everlasting. It was the foundation of man's security, and by its principles God directed how man should
live as well as what he should believe. The Temple was a central symbol but Temple activities were directed by the Law,
not vice versa.

Folk tales such as Judith and Tobit graphically illustrate
the meaning of the good life under the Law. Doing deeds of
kindness was a central theme in the life of Tobit who, though
an exile in a foreign land, maintained the Law faithfully in
all his doings. Tobit built his life on prayer, alms-giving, and
fasting (Tobit 12:8). While these were external works, there
was a deep sense of piety which was the inner stimulus for
keeping the Law. In the Testament of Joseph the patriarch
tells how he fended off the advances of Potiphar's wife by
prayer and fasting (9:1–10:2). Keeping the Law involved

acts of devotional performance in private life as well as deeds of kindness in daily relationships and cultic performance at the Temple. Even when kindness brought grief as it did to Tobit, the ultimate result was joy and peace.

Judith is a bloody story whose heroine, a widow, fulfilled the law of mourning for her husband, yet she kept the feasts and Sabbaths. Even in the Gentile camp, she ate alone and had kosher food in keeping with the regulations of God.

The great principles of Law and the fixed ideas of cult raised real conflicts of interest and understanding in the minds of sensitive and thoughtful people. Many wise men in Israel became scribes after Ezra's time and were the official interpreters of the Law. Prophetic vision gave way to scribal interpretation. When a question arose about faith or life, it was not settled by the insight of a prophet or the answer of a priest, but the scribe was often called to provide an answer. To keep the Law was primary; hence detailed knowledge became indispensable. This led to endless discussions and to voluminous commentaries directed to detailed answers.

A mixture of worldly wisdom with prescriptions for keeping the Law of God came into being because of the urgent need to keep the Law in every exact detail. Wisdom was a practical, commonsense approach to life and the world, drawn from the total experience of mankind. The Jews equated the Law of Moses with this international material on religion, manners, and morals. Wisdom was said to be the key to the good life. For the Jews, therefore, keeping the Law and following Wisdom were identical.

For the Son of Sirach, keeping the Law meant following good manners and exercising good sense in all of life's activities. To live in this manner was also the fulfillment of Wisdom.[7]

Law was said to be God's eternal decree for man's faith and life, but in the apocryphal and pseudepigraphical works Wisdom was personified sometimes as a woman to be sought after and sometimes as God active in man's world. Wisdom was an intermediate power by which man came into a knowledge of God. When personified, Wisdom became privy to all the secrets of God and was the best possible teacher about God. Whether personified as a beautiful and desirable woman or as the active, creative spirit of God, Wisdom became far more than an accumulation of wise sayings. In fact, during the last two centuries before Christ, it was held that Wisdom existed before creation; by Wisdom all things were created and through Wisdom God's will acted in the world.

Both Law and Wisdom in recorded form tended to become static religious principles which required constant interpretation. From a legalistic basis, scribes sought to bring Law and Wisdom to bear on every phase of living. Spiritual freedom gave way before religious requirement and the creative sources of faith were imperiled.

Having said this about the aphorisms and legalistic interpretations of Wisdom, we hasten to add that wise men and scribes came to grips with some of the thorny problems of religious thought and practice. While their insights may appear doctrinaire and wooden to us, in their day they represented movement and searching for meaning within the structures of cult, the situations of normal life, and the instruction of the Law. We are in their debt, but the future dynamic of faith was not provided by them; it had to come from other sources.

Basis for Hope and the Coming Kingdom

Eschatology developed rapidly in this period with various changes and interchanges in patterns of its expression. Hope among the Jews had always appeared within the framework of a full future restoration of the twelve tribes to their former glory (Test. of Judah 25:1-2). A new Israel was forecast before the Hasmonean period, but in the disappointment of the latter days of that period the new Israel remained an unrealized hope. The form of expectation continued to be an earthly empire with men living for a thousand years and begetting many children.

Another structure of hope thrust its foundations deeper into the past and became a regular feature of any future. After Beliar and his dark minions were cleared off the earth, the saints of God would themselves be restored to New Jerusalem and returned to Eden. Apparently future hope was to be expressed in terms of return to an original paradisal state or to the highest and the best experienced in history. Whether this New Jerusalem was on earth or was supermundane is not an easy problem to decide on the basis of available evidence. There probably was an unresolved ambiguity left in the minds of the writers as well as the readers who produced the documents of the times which are our source material.

Resurrection was an accepted fact, and beyond resurrection the judgment of God upon Jews and upon Gentiles was confidently expected. According to the literature of the day, all the early Jewish patriarchs would be raised at the last day. Following Daniel's lead, faithful Jews believed in resurrection of the just to a reward and the unjust to punishment. In this situation embryonic doctrines of heaven and hell are held for the moment of full growth.

Hope and expectation were related to the belief that God would send his messiah or the son of man to bring in the ultimate Kingdom. The kingdoms of men would dissolve before the Kingdom of God, which would be brought in by the messiahs of Levi and Judah. In other words, sacred and secular messiahs would be sent to set up God's order in the created universe. In the Zadokite Fragment, and to some extent in several of the Dead Sea Scrolls, the same division of messianic function is felt.

This messianic kingdom was to be set up on earth with priestly and princely functions carried on by the messiahs of Levi and Judah. This dual role eventually coalesced into a single messiah. The new Israel of faith, whether under one messiah or two, would be brought to the earth under God through messianic rule. That day was expected to dawn on those faithful Essenes who kept the Law in community and built brotherhood in the desert where they chose to live at Qumran. Fulfillment of the exact requirements of the Law would hasten, if not bring about, the day of the messiah's coming to his true people.

A subtle change occurred during this period when the idea of a messiah who had been the appointed vice-regent of God became in fact the son of man, a super-human being. This son of man, as delineated in Enoch, pre-existed from the beginning (Enoch 48:2). His dominion was absolutely universal (Enoch 62:6) and the judgment of God was given into his hands to execute (Enoch 69:27). He was a heavenly being in contrast to the earthly nature of the traditional messiah. Jesus later identified himself with the son of man who would come on clouds of glory and with the suffering servant figure in Second Isaiah. Just how far Jesus was influenced by the figure of the son of man in Enoch remains a question. But that he was aware of such a figure as depicted in Enoch should not be denied. He was certainly fulfilling the mission of Israel who is depicted as a corporate son of man in Daniel.[8]

The promise of God to re-establish Israel to a dominant position in the earth began to break out of its cocoon and be conceived of as something more. The promise became not that of man restored to his rightful place in a renewed society but of man risen from the dead living in a new heaven and a new earth. Individual resurrection was conceived in purely spiritual terms; that is, the soul was kept alive and the body was cast off. This attitude stems directly from the influence on Hebrew thought of the Greek idea of separating body and spirit.

The kingdom of God became a Kingdom of heaven in which the saints, risen and purified, would live in perfect light. Between death and life a waiting place, an intermediate state, was also provided for the individual. Sheol was chosen to be the resting place for those who waited God's great day of judgment. At the end time God would separate the sons of darkness from the sons of light. Heaven was the place of the righteous, and hell became the abode of the wicked. Evil had no further power or contact with goodness.

A coalescence of individual and community hope occurred in some such manner as we have described. Neither individual nor corporate hope was lost—both were held inviolate. In early Israel, future hope dealt almost exclusively with the future of the community and the nation. Events, however, put a real strain on this exclusive, corporate concept of continuance when the people were scattered in exile. Quite simply, hope became more individualized in the exilic and postexilic periods. Yet the Greek idea of self-centered man, immortal in himself, never gained a permanent foothold in Hebrew thought. Individuals were raised to new life in a new Kingdom of heaven. Hope apart from community was an unthinkable concept to the Hebrew mind even after considerable change due to the impact of Greek thought.

At the end of history, hope and expectation were that God, who had created a force of light and a force of darkness, would destroy the darkness. Beliar would be bound and cast into a fiery pit together with all other fallen spirits. The son of man would then appear to take over the rule of all the earth and restore the kingdom to God's faithful people. The earthly bounds of future hope were set for a definite period of time, but after that the restored earthly kingdom would become a heavenly realm. (This has become grist for the mill of millenarians in New Testament studies.) By this device the whole contradiction of restored earthly kingdom versus strictly heavenly Kingdom was resolved or at least suspended.

God's victory and rule would be complete in that day both on earth and in heaven. Some writers saw the advent of the Kingdom in gradual terms as in Jubilees 4:25; 23:26-28, while others foresaw a great castastrophic event as in Daniel 2 and 8, and Enoch 83-90. In either case the power and triumph of the Almighty were absolutely sure. (Later in the New Testament one detects a blending of the gradual coming and the catastrophic appearance of the Kingdom among men. This is especially the case with the teachings of Jesus as reflected in the Synoptic Gospels.)

When God's victory occurred, his saints who kept the Law, making prayer and sacrifice, giving alms and doing kindness, were to be rewarded for their goodness. The righteous dead were to rise to life in a new Kingdom of heaven; they would reign with God over the new order of creation which was supermundane and was in fact heaven. It was the region of the blessed whether on earth or in heaven or in both.

Hell, as we have pointed out earlier, was derived from the idea that Beliar would be bound and cast into a pit. All the sons of darkness, whether fallen angels or evil men, would join him. Whether they were to suffer extinction there or to suffer perpetually remains a moot point in the creative era prior to the time of Jesus. In due time the valley of Hinnom near Jerusalem came into the picture. Gehenna (Hebrew *gan-hinnom*, Greek *ge-henna*) became a hell for the wicked. Fire was borrowed from the Zoroastrian influence and soon the division in this world became permanent in the world to come.

The dualistic nature of the present universe, seen and unseen, was to be healed in the future ideal world when the two were to be made one. Disruption by evil would be stopped; God's authority would no longer be challenged by evil nor would his light be made dim by the darkness. In the world to come, the struggle was over; evil had lost all its power to destroy righteousness.

Against this shifting background of future hope and confident expectation, men and women were called to live out their lives in faith. Suffering could be redemptive or just a trial of faith, but it was a temporary situation for the faithful. Even though Tobit suffered greatly in his righteousness, still the grace and goodness of God delivered him out of reach of all ultimate or permanent harm. So also the prose ending to Job gave promise that suffering would be but for a short time and then reward would come.

At this time there came a man out of Galilee preaching the gospel and saying, "The kingdom of God is at hand; repent, and believe in the gospel." Of himself he said, "I am the light of the world." In him the end time had come, the last age had dawned.

Conclusion

The Gospel of God

Jesus came proclaiming "the good news" that the Kingdom of God was at hand. He invited his listeners by faith to enter into that Kingdom which was now open to all men. It superseded the kingdoms of this world and was not to be equated with the kingdom of Israel or the varied concepts of the kingdom in this period. Repentance was "a change of mind" on the basis of the evidence that the Kingdom of God was at hand.

Jesus of Nazareth was more concerned with the will of God than he was with his mission for God; therefore, we have no clear explanation of that mission in his own words. Despite the scarcity of evidence, however, we may conclude from the Synoptic Gospels that Jesus patterned his life after the figure of the suffering servant in Isaiah and the son of man as described in Daniel. This mixture of the two missions is nowhere better seen than in the dialogue with Caiaphas, the high priest, during the trial of Jesus. The high priest asked in urgent accent: "I adjure you by the living God, tell us if you are the Christ, the son of God" (Matt. 26:63b). And Jesus answered, "You have said so. But I tell you, hereafter you will see the Son of man seated at the right hand of Power, and coming on the clouds of heaven" (Matt. 26:64). Earlier, following the same approach, Jesus promised his hearers, "Truly, I say to you, there are some standing here who will not taste death before they see the Son of man coming in his kingdom" (Matt. 16:28). It is the same Son of Man who is Lord of the Sabbath and who can expand or deepen the meaning of Law as it applies to Sabbath observance (Mark 2:27-28). Jesus joined his mission of suffering with that of the triumphant Son of Man when he said, "The Son of man must suffer many things, and be rejected by the elders and chief priests and scribes, and be killed, and on the third day be raised" (Luke 9:22). ". . . the Son of man came not to be served but to serve, and to give his life as a ransom for many" (Matt. 20:28). There can be little doubt that Jesus patterned his life and mission along these lines. In Jesus Christ the Son of Man had come to be the Suffering Servant for the sins of men.

Jesus believed and taught that God had power over all powers both seen and unseen. He was unimpressed by the societies and organizations of men. Man's first duty was to the Kingdom of God. When Jesus taught his followers to render unto Caesar the things that were Caesar's, he was at odds with the Zealots, and when he liberalized the Law, he went directly counter to the Pharisees and Essenes.

Being a Jew, Jesus understood the spirit and meaning of the Law which from its inception rested on two primary pillars: love for God and love for one's neighbor. Multitudes of rules had blurred the underlying spirit and purpose of God's Law, but this original intent was recovered in some of the teachings gathered together in the Sermon on the Mount. In his sayings Jesus dug down below the level of consciousness in man to the motive centers. To not murder a man was insufficient; nor was it enough to refrain from hatred. Love was the Law. What did love mean? Doubtless there was a vast literature on the subject, but Jesus described love and the meaning of being a neighbor in the incomparable story of the Good Samaritan. The Law was directed not only at the content of life; it also had to do with the intent of life. Motivation was the criterion for measuring righteousness. Love for God and love for neighbor was the whole Law and the prophets.

Jesus had come into the world to inaugurate the Kingdom of God among men; but the Kingdom had neither fully nor finally come. A new age had begun, yet the new age was not fulfilled, so Jesus could pray, "Thy kingdom come" (Matt. 6:10), and at the same time say, "the kingdom of God is in the midst of you" (Luke 17:21). But with the coming of Jesus, what Daniel saw of the kingdoms of earth replaced by the Kingdom of heaven began to happen. The Kingdom had come, was coming, and was to come.

Our Lord was the King of the Jews and any who chose to follow him. Perhaps it was because of misunderstanding of his language that he was actually mistaken for a revolutionary by the Romans. Yet he said plainly, "My kingship is not of this world . . . " (John 18:36). He indicated that if his Kingdom were of this world his disciples would fight. Jesus did not foresee a kingdom on the earth, although he foresaw the time when his twelve apostles would sit on twelve thrones (Matt. 19:28). One wonders if Jesus ever expected a restoration of the Jewish kingdom in Judah, centered around Jerusalem.

The manifestation of the power of God was measured by the forces, seen and unseen, over which God held power. Jesus held sway over the forces of nature and could still a storm at sea. He held power over sickness and could restore a person from death to life, according to the record. But his primary struggle was against the unseen powers of the air.

In temptation in the desert, Jesus fought the battle of the soul against the unseen enemy who attacked. The attack was mounted, as in the Garden of Eden, with great subtlety and suggestiveness. The three temptations passed and were answered from a thorough knowledge of the ancient Scriptures. And when the demonic forces had done their worst, then "angels came and ministered to him" (Matt. 4:11). The divided world of struggle was the one to which Jesus came.

He recognized the demonic basis for illness, the most popular explanation for the cause of sickness at the time. Exorcism was part of his mission. An epileptic boy was cured when the evil spirit was called out of him (Luke 9:37-43) and a Gerasene madman regained his sanity when the spirit which had long troubled him was cast out (Mark 5:1-20). Jesus proclaimed his triumphant power by saying that not only was he not in league with the devil, but he had bound the devil and had gained power over his domain (Mark 4:

20-27). Jesus had gained power over evil in its several mani-
festations. The dawn of the new age had come.

But the gospel of God involved the death and resurrection of Jesus, who proclaimed himself the Son of Man. His
crucifixion was the demonstration of God's love to men and
was the creative suffering in which men were made new again.
God's own action released man from his condition. Forgiveness
was wrought by what God did.

The gospel binds up the pieces of expressed hope and
desperation, making them into a pattern of God's intervention on man's behalf. It marks the beginning of the end of
darkness and evil in the world. The basic battle had been
fought and won by Jesus Christ, and men were invited by
faith to enter into the fruits of his victory. Meanwhile, he
was and remains the Lord of history and the Master of life.
Men live under the power and grace of God and wait in
confidence for the final manifestation. Life is made new and
eternal in union with Christ.

The church used the prepared stage to proclaim the
drama of God's act in Christ and to call men into the new
Kingdom of love. Behavior was cast in the verbiage of earlier times but was radically different in content. Hope was
expressed in terms of the defeat of evil unseen forces and
the establishment of one Kingdom of love and light. God's
ultimate triumph was partly realized already but partly expected still. The gospel of God was that God is active in a
changing universe. Men are called to participation in God's
activity, having been given freedom through God's forgiveness.

The creative era gave way to the cosmic, creative act of
God in Jesus Christ. Paul expressed the result of God's activity in these familiar words: "Therefore, if any one is in
Christ, he is a new creation; the old has passed away, behold,
the new has come" (2 Cor. 5:17). New creations were called
to put on the whole armor of God and to fight against world
rulers of darkness in the confidence that these forces were already
defeated and the darkness was passing away.

Notes and Acknowledgments

CHAPTER I

1. James B. Pritchard, *Ancient Near Eastern Texts Relating to the Old Testament* (Princeton: Princeton University Press, 1950), pp. 315-316.

2. William F. Albright, "The Biblical Period," from *The Jews: Their History, Culture, and Religion*, Vol. I, ed. Louis Finkelstein (New York: Harper & Brothers, Publishers, 1949), pp. 3-65.

3. Darius I was a great ruler and a masterful administrator who left an indelible imprint of organizational pattern on the Persian Empire. Cyrus and Cambyses had been primarily military men who spent their main effort on conquest and gave little attention to organization. After their reigns the sprawling new empire was still not organized. The task of organization fell to Darius who was well equipped to do it. Local princes such as Zerubbabel were replaced by district governors in the new pattern. This reform was made because local native governors often fomented revolts against central authority. Darius divided the empire into twenty districts or satrapies over each of which he appointed a civilian governor and an independent military officer responsible, not to the governor, but to the great king himself. This system did much to strengthen the empire and to forestall any plans for local autonomy in Judah or elsewhere. It also probably accounts for the removal and disappearance of Zerubbabel from the scene. Cf. W. O. E. Oesterley, *A History of Israel*, Vol. II (Oxford: Oxford University Press, 1932), pp. 67-68.

4. Wallace Everett Caldwell, *The Ancient World* (New York: Rinehart & Company, Inc., 1937), pp. 186-190.

5. There is massive evidence on this subject. Nehemiah built the walls which Ezra found when he arrived (Ezra 9:9). Nehemiah's marriage reform would seem to have little meaning if Ezra's work were already done. The high priest who was a contemporary of Nehemiah

was Eliashib (Neh. 3:1) but Ezra lived in the time of Jehohanan who was the grandson of Eliashib (Ezra 10:6; Neh. 12:10, 22). In Nehemiah 7:4, Jerusalem is described as being thinly populated, but Ezra 10:1 reflects a very different state of affairs. Yet it appears that the lives of the two men overlap and complement one another. Therefore, the best solution to a difficult problem is to accept the textual error, reading "thirty-seventh" year instead of "seventh," and dating Ezra's ministry from 428 B.C., not 458 B.C. For an extensive discussion of the problem, cf. H. H. Rowley, *Nehemiah's Mission and Its Background* (Manchester: The John Rylands Library, 1955).

6. Neither Athens nor Sparta presented an offensive threat to the Persians, although they had turned back Persian invasions. Within the Persian Empire in its declining years, three major rulers followed Artaxerxes I to the throne. After a time of uncertainty in dynastic succession, Darius II (423-404 B.C.) gained ascendency, to be followed by Artaxerxes II (404-358 B.C.). He in turn was succeeded by Artaxerxes III (358-338 B.C.). Darius III (338-331 B.C.) was the last ruler of a waning and weak empire. Cf. Oesterley, *op. cit.*, pp. 63-70. A more detailed history of Persia is to be found in Albert T. Olmstead's *History of the Persian Empire* (Chicago: The University of Chicago Press, 1948).

7. The origin of the term "Hasmonean" is somewhat uncertain but is said to be the name of an ancestor of Mattathias. It could be a place name, but the term refers to the Hasmonean dynasty which began with Simon and actually ended when Rome took over in 63 B.C. However, the house continued in the high priesthood for some time. Herod finally wiped out the line.

CHAPTER II

1. Cf. works of Flavius Josephus, including *The Antiquities of the Jews* and *The Wars of the Jews* which can be found in a number of different publications.

2. An excellent summary and analysis of the Old Testament Apocrypha is given in Bruce M. Metzger, *An Introduction to the Apocrypha* (New York: Oxford University Press, 1957), pp. 3-150, and also in R. H. Pfeiffer, *History of New Testament Times* (New York: Harper & Brothers Publishers, 1949), pp. 233-522. These two works, together with the Revised Standard Version of the Apocrypha, furnish needed material for additional study.

3. Cf. Pfeiffer, *op. cit.*, pp. 354-364.

4. Pfeiffer, *op. cit.*, pp. 76-77.

5. For additional study, see R. H. Charles, *The Apocrypha and Pseudepigrapha*, Vol. II (Oxford: Oxford University Press, 1913); also H. H. Rowley, *The Relevance of the Apocalyptic* (London: Lutterworth Press, 1944); also Pfeiffer, *op. cit.*, pp. 60-90.

6. For additional reading on the Dead Sea Scrolls we recommend Millar Burrows, *The Dead Sea Scrolls* (New York: The Viking Press, 1955) and *More Light on the Dead Sea Scrolls* (New York: The Viking Press, 1958); Frank Cross, *The Ancient Library of Qumran and Modern Biblical Studies*, rev. ed. (Garden City, N. Y.: Doubleday, 1961); Yigael Yadin, *The Message of the Scrolls* (New York: Simon and Schuster, 1957); and Krister Stendahl, ed., *The Scrolls and the New Testament* (New York: Harper and Brothers, 1957).

7. Cf. Theodor H. Gaster, *The Dead Sea Scriptures* (Garden City, N. Y.: Doubleday, 1958), pp. 39-60.

CHAPTER III

1. Cf. Günther Bornkamm, *Jesus of Nazareth*, tr. Irene and Fraser McLuskey (New York: Harper & Brothers, Publishers, 1960), p. 39.

2. Cf. Robert C. Dentan, *The Apocrypha, Bridge of the Testaments* (Greenwich: The Seabury Press, 1954), p. 32.

3. Sherman Johnson, *Jesus in His Homeland* (New York: Charles Scribner's Sons, 1957), pp. 10-16.

4. Pfeiffer, *op. cit.*, p. 56.

5. The four philosophies mentioned by Josephus in his works *The Wars of the Jews* and *The Antiquities of the Jews* were Pharisees, Sadducees, Essenes, and Zealots.

6. Charles, *op. cit.*, pp. 785 ff.

7. Cf. Jean Daniélou, *The Dead Sea Scrolls and Primitive Christianity*, tr. Salvator Attanasio (Baltimore: Helicon Press, Inc., 1958), pp. 25-37.

8. For an excellent discussion of the Zealots and Jesus, see Johnson, *op. cit.*, pp. 89-110.

9. Cf. William Reuben Farmer, *Maccabees, Zealots, and Josephus* (New York: Columbia University Press, 1956), for enlightening study on the spiritual continuum from Maccabees to Zealots.

10. Yadin, *op. cit.*, pp. 128-143

CHAPTER IV

1. For a thorough discussion of temptation understood in this way,

see "New Light on Temptation, Sin, and Flesh in the New Testament" in Stendahl, *op. cit.*, pp. 94-113.

2. Cf. Pfeiffer, *op. cit.*, pp. 49-50.

3. Pfeiffer, *op. cit.*, pp. 179-181.

4. For further discussion of the synagogue, see Norman H. Smith, *The Jews From Cyrus to Herod* (New York: Abingdon Press, 1957), pp. 190-194; also George Foote Moore, *Judaism*, Vol. I, in *The First Centuries of the Christian Era* (Cambridge: Harvard University Press, 1927), pp. 281-307.

CHAPTER V

1. Burrows, *op. cit.*, p. 374.

2. *Ibid.*, p. 375

3. *Ibid.*, p. 376.

4. For a discussion of the date of Daniel, see Rowley, *op. cit.*, pp. 11-50.

5. For the literary and historical sources of Daniel, cf. C. G. Howie, *Ezekiel and Daniel*, Layman's Bible Commentary, Vol. 13 (Richmond: John Knox Press, 1961), pp. 89-92.

6. Rowley, *op. cit.*, pp. 27-30.

7. Pfeiffer, *op. cit.*, p. 405.

8. The writer cannot agree with T. W. Manson that Jesus was unaware of the son of man idea in Enoch. Cf. T. W. Manson, *The Son of Man in Daniel, Enoch and the Gospels* (reprinted from *Bulletin of the John Rylands Library*, Vol. 32, No. 2, March 1950), pp. 171-193.

ALETHEIA Paperbacks are carefully selected for use in personal or group study. Titles in the expanding series range in subject matter from theology for laymen to church history, Bible study, and Christian living.

CARL G. HOWIE is minister of Calvary Presbyterian Church, San Francisco, California. A graduate of Lees McRae and Davidson Colleges, he received B.D. and Th.M. degrees from Union Theological Seminary in Virginia and a Ph.D. from Johns Hopkins University. He is the author of **The Dead Sea Scrolls and the Living Church, God in the Eternal Present,** and the volume on Ezekiel and Daniel in the **Layman's Bible Commentary.**

THE CREATIVE ERA: BETWEEN THE TESTAMENTS. The obscure but exciting period between the Testaments is a blank for many people who are otherwise well versed in Bible history. Yet we must understand the happenings of these four centuries if we are to grasp the meaning of the New Testament.

These were the years when the Persians came and went, when the Greeks left their indelible imprint on the minds of men, when the Romans rose to power. As for the Jews, the flexibility of their theological viewpoints encouraged creative thinking. Pharisees, Sadducees, Essenes, Zealots, and other sects emerged.

Against the historical backdrop of this formative period, Carl G. Howie traces the thought patterns which became the framework for Jesus' ideas and teachings. Drawing on such records as the Old Testament, Apocrypha, Pseudepigrapha, and Dead Sea Scrolls, he colorfully portrays one of mankind's most significant eras and shows how it served as prologue to God's revelation in Jesus Christ.